Gog and Magog.

THE TAILOR'S GIANT,
SALISBURY.

Gog and Magog.

THE

GIANTS IN GUILDHALL;

Their real and legendary History.

WITH AN ACCOUNT OF OTHER CIVIC GIANTS, AT
HOME AND ABROAD.

BY F. W. FAIRHOLT, F.S.A.

HONORARY MEMBER OF THE SOCIETIES OF ANTIQUARIES OF NORMANDY, PICARDY
AND POITIERS.

WITH ILLUSTRATIONS BY THE AUTHOR.

ARMS OF ANTWERP.

LONDON:
JOHN CAMDEN HOTTEN, PICCADILLY.

1859.

PREFACE.

THE present volume,—a small contri-
bution to the civic history of our
metropolis,—has grown out of a brief
lecture I read in the summer of the
present year, at the meeting of the
London and Middlesex Archæological
Association, in Guildhall. The foundation was laid by Hone, the only
writer who seems to have cared to
devote more than a passing word to the
giants, who have always been popular

favourites. Speaking of his own feeling on this subject (which the writer shares with him), he says: "From the time when I was astonished by the information, that 'every day when the giants hear the clock strike twelve, they come down to dinner,' I have had something of curiosity towards them. How came they there, and what are they for? In vain have been my examinations of Stow, Havel, Strype, Noorthouck, Maitland, Seymour, Pennant, and numberless other authors of books and tracts, regarding London. They scarcely deign to mention them." To Hone's notes I have added much on their early legendary history; their public appearances on great festive occasions (such as royal entries to London, and Mayoralty shows); many literary notices which escaped him; and, more particularly, such a descriptive account of continental giants as illustrates the position our Guildhall giants once held; and which have not before been brought to bear on their history, although, as I fully believe, their origin must be sought in that direction.

Modern commerce owes an eternal debt of gratitude for its very existence, to the determined resistance of the traders of the middle ages to an effete and destructive feudalism. The true history of trade is the real history of modern civilization. It had its martyrs

in the adventurous men of the Low
Countries, who ultimately triumphed, and
fixed on a firm basis the rights of the
commercial community. Their clear-
headed wisdom saw a new field for
prosperous industry; and glorious was
the triumph achieved. The magnificent
hotels-de-ville of their ancient towns, tell
of the mine of wealth opened to the
middle classes. The people's *fétes* on
great occasions rivalled the royal and
nobler festivals, which at one time were
confined to the aristocracy. It is in
their popular displays we find the origin
of our own ancient civic observances;
and it is curious to note how exactly
they were copied to the minutest point.
The history of English trade and muni-

cipal pageantry can never be complete without this reference to continental usages.

The addenda to this volume is of a nature with the *Pièces Justificatives*, which foreign antiquaries so frequently and so usefully append to their works, as proofs of the authenticity of their text, or as indications to the reader for further researches.

My object has been to touch lightly on this whole subject; but at the same time to indicate the profound antiquity of the popular belief in giants. The sacred, as well as the classic authors confirm this belief; and if Polyphemus be forgotten, Goliath is well-remembered. Many striking localities are associated with the gigantic heroes of the middle ages : the rock known as "Arthur's Seat," at Edinburgh ; and that termed "the Chair of Gargantua," on the Seine, preserve popular tradition. The Colossal Statuary of Egypt, Greece, and Rome, may have had its effect in strengthening the belief of the Gothic tribes who rose to power upon the decay of Roman greatness. The enormous wicker figures in which human victims were sacrificed to the barbaric gods, have by some au- thors been considered as the prototypes of the wicker-giants paraded at home and abroad in civic festivities. This was the opinion enforced by Dr. Milner,

the historian of Winchester, but one
which the author of the present volume
thinks it needless to dwell exclusively
upon; as enough will have been said
in the course of it to show the universality
of belief held by the people of all ages
and countries in a gigantic race, enemies
to those of ordinary stature.

Not wishing to succumb to Dr.
Johnson, Charles Lamb, or Letitia
Landon, in attachment to the great
capital of which he is a native, the
author dedicates this little volume to
genuine lovers of London and its history,
as " a quaint chapter of half-forgotten
lore;" happy if they will sit (like
Mistress Quickly) " at the latter end of

a sea-coal fire," and kindly devote an hour to an unpretentious fellow citizen, who will gossip on " thinges olde."

F. W. FAIRHOLT.

11, MONTPELIER SQUARE,

    BROMPTON,

        DECEMBER, 1859.

Illustrations.

—•◦•—

The Guildhall Giants.

---◦◦✦◦✦◦◦---

MYTHOLOGY has always usurped the place
of sober history in the popular mind. The
ancestry of all peoples, by its means, were
connected with the Gods, or were supposed
superhuman in size or power. In early art,
as in early story, great characters were lite-
rally great of body. The gods and kings of
early Egypt were giants among men, when
sculptured or painted on the storied walls of
the temples and palaces of that mystic land.
The national heroes of Greece and Rome
were endowed with gigantic frames. Hero-

dotus tells of the footstep of Hercules shown in Scythia, and the sandal of Perseus found at Chemnis, as being both two cubits in length. The Gothic nations indulged the same exaggerated belief of their godlike and gigantic ancestry. The heroes of Knight-errantry were similarly vast. Of the King Arthur, Higden desires us (when speaking of the discovery of his body at Glastonbury) to " have mynde that Arthures chyn-bone, that was thenne shewed, was longer by three inches than the legge and the knee of the largest man that was then found. Also the face of his forehead, by-tweene hys two eyen, was a spanne broad." The grave of Sir Gawain, one of his far-famed Knights of the Round Table, was fourteen feet in length. Another hero, Sir Bevis, of Hamton, is still depicted as a giant on the bar-gate, at Southampton; and the

renowned Guy of Warwick is popularly supposed to have left personal relics at Warwick
Castle sufficient to prove his vast stature.
His breastplate, weighing 52lbs., is there
shewn to strengthen the belief of the faith-
ful, who will not see that it is the crupper of
a horse as used in the sixteenth century.
Guy's "porridge-pot," capable of holding
102 gallons, it is a species of sacrilege to
look on only as a large camp kettle. The
author has a vivid remembrance of the in-
dignation with which his translation of these
"genuine relics" was received in Warwick
some few years ago. It was like daring to
doubt the liquefaction of the blood of St. Jan-
uarius in Naples, or the truth of the holy coat
at Treves. When such things remain with
us to confirm in our own time the fables of
past ages, we may qualify our surprise at
the head of a crocodile passing at Mons for

B 2

that of the dragon slain by the redoubtable
Gilles-de-Chin; or the bones of whales and
extinct animals for those of "monstrous
giants." It is a popular fallacy willingly
believed, and desired to be confided in.*

Giants were always great favourites with
the commonalty, and entered very largely
into the fabulous histories of the middle
ages, whether they were early histories of a
country, lives of the saints, or tales of
chivalry. It was, consequently, no unusual
thing to introduce them in tournaments,
and thus, in some degree, realize the older

* Stow notes, that in the Church of St. Lawrence,
Jury, was "the shank-bone of a man (as it is taken),
and also a tooth of very great bigness hanged up for
show in chains of iron, upon a pillar of stone; the tooth
(being about the bigness of a man's fist) is long since
conveyed from thence; the shank-bone, of 25 inches in
length, remaineth yet, fastened to a post of timber."
He very sensibly considers the tooth might be that "of
some monstrous fish;" and the leg-bone, "of an elephant."

knightly battles. In the German *Thurnier-Buchs* of the sixteenth century, gigantic figures sometimes mix in the *melée*.

This popular love of giants, led the municipalities of many cities in Flanders and Belgium to provide figures of the kind for grand fête days. Thus Antwerp, Louvain, Malines, Asselt, Brussels, Ath, Ghent, Bruges, Tournay, Lille, Dunkirk, Ypres, Poperinghe, Cassel, Douai, &c., have each their communal giant, which, upon certain days, is carried about these towns. They are constructed in various styles, and habited in still more varied costumes, ranging from the Roman (as at Antwerp) to the court dress of the last century (as at Brussels). Sometimes they are formed of osier, as at Cassel, Hazebrouck, and Asselt ; sometimes of elaborate wood-carving of a fine and expensive kind, as at Antwerp.

In directing attention therefore to the carved figures which so strikingly decorate the old Guildhall of London, it will be necessary to carry our researches far beyond the comparatively recent period at which they were fabricated ; to look a little at the Guild observances of the great continental trading towns; as well as take a retrospective glance at the once-popular fabulous history of the early foundation of London.

In the old days when the inventions of the Monkish Chronicler, or the still more fanciful Romancist, or Minstrel Bard, were seriously listened to as history ; it became part of the popular belief that the original name of London was New Troy, and that it was founded by Brute or Brutus, the younger son of Anthenor of Troy; who, when that city was sacked by the Greeks, fled to Italy, and founded the city of Pavia, from whence

his son, in search of new conquests, voyaged
around the Spanish and French coasts,
obtained the aid of the Gauls to invade
Britain, and landed in the port where now
Southampton stands.

Let us now see by whom he was opposed.
Caxton, in his *Chronicle of England*, seriously prints, what the old authors as
seriously wrote, about the first peopling of
this island. It is to this effect. The
Emperor Dioclesian had three and thirty
self-willed daughters, of whose management
he was at last relieved by obtaining for them
as many husbands. But the ladies did not
pleasantly submit to the rule of their lords,
and agreed among themselves to regain their
lost liberties by each cutting her husband's
throat. The deed was effected, and the
Emperor their father, driven to despair of
managing so refractory a family, to punish

their crimes, and rid himself of their presence, sent all to sea in one vessel with half a year's provisions. After long sailing they reached an island, which they made their residence, and named *Albion*, after the name of the eldest lady. The Evil One, who never lost sight of them, created visionary husbands for these ladies, who became the mothers of " horrible giants," and they ruled in the land until the advent of Brutus.

We now arrive at "the veritable history" of our Guildhall Giants, included in his invasion, as thus given in the history of the Trojan wars, sold cheaply to the people as late as 1735.*   The Giant son of the above lady in this version names our Island.

---

* *The History of the Trojan Wars, and Troy's De-struction.* London, printed for Sarah Bates, at the Sun and Bible, in Giltspur Street ; and James Hodges, at the Looking Glass, on London Bridge. 12mo. 1735.

"Brute, having thus got footing in Britain, was preparing to improve the same, when Albion, who had named this island after his own name,—by which it is sometimes called at this day,—having intelligence thereof, raised his whole power, being men of a gigantick stature, and vast strength, and bearing for their arms huge clubs of knotty oak, battle axes, whirlbats of iron, and globes full of spikes, fastened to a long pole by a chain; and with these encountering Brute, a bloody battle was fought, wherein the Trojans were worsted and many of them slain, and their whole army was forced to retire.

" Brute hereupon considering the disadvantage between his men and the giants, devised a stratagem to overthrow them, by digging in the night a very long and deep trench, at the bottom impaling it with

sharp stakes, and covering it with boughs
and rotten hurdles, on which he caused to
be laid dried leaves and earth, only leaving
some firm passages, well known to his men
by particular marks.

" This being done, he dared the giants
to a second battle, which Albion readily
accepted; and the fight being begun, after
some dispute, Brute seemed to retire; where-
upon the giants pressed on him with great
fury; and the Trojans retiring nimbly beyond their trench, made a stand, and ply'd
them with a shower of darts and arrows,
which manner of fight they were unac-
quainted with, whereby many of them
were slain. However, Albion encouraging
his men to come to handy strokes with
their enemies, they rushed forward, and
the vanguard immediately perished in the
trenches; and the Trojans continuing to

shoot their arrows very thick, the giants were put to flight, and pursued into Cornwall; where, in another bloody fight, Albion was slain by Brute, fighting hand to hand; and his two brothers, Gog and Magog, giants of huge stature, were taken prisoners and led in triumph to the place where now London stands, and upon those risings on the side of the river Thames, founded a city, which he called *Troy-novant*, or *New Troy*, and building a palace where Guildhall stands, caused the two giants to be chained to the gate of it, as porters. In memory of which it is held that their effigies, after their deaths, were set up as they now appear in Guildhall."

This quotation will show how completely the figures of these giants accord with the description of them here given; "the globe full of spikes, fastened to a long pole by

a chain," is carried by the elder figure.
Though this weapon be not as ancient as
the era fixed by this veritable history as
that in which the giants flourished, it be-
longs to the mediæval era, and was named
"a Morning Star;" being used by horse-
men to whirl about them in the *melée*, and
break the armour, or otherwise injure,
fighting men.

It might be thought scarcely worth the
student's while to recur to what many may
think absurdities, had not these absurdities
been gravely recorded and produced as
veritable histories by our ancestors, and
did we not to this day preserve their dream-
ings in visible figures of the giants thus
conquered.   These tales were so much
valued by our forefathers that they were
transcribed as well authenticated and sober
early history in their *Liber Albus*, as well

as in the *Recordatorium Civitatis Speculum*; and advanced in a memorial presented to Henry VI, and now preserved in the Tower of London, as an evidence of "the Great Antiquity, precedency, and dignity of the City of London, even before Rome." This foundation of London having taken place, according to Geoffrey of Monmouth, about the year of the World 2885, or 1008 years before the birth of Christ.

In the old tragedy of *Locrine*, once attributed to Shakespeare, the same story is detailed, and "stately Troynovant" mentioned as the principal city of Albion, and the burial place of Brute, or Brutus, after his life of adventure. The victory over the giants is alluded to by him in the first scene of this play, where he details the history of his wanderings from Troy, until

> " ————————upon the strands of Albion
> To Corus haven happily we came,
> And quell'd the giants, come of Albion's race,
> With Gogmagog, son to Samotheus,
> The cursed captain of that damned crew."

The name therefore of one of these giants has been split into two, and we now call one Gog and the other Magog. The names originally were Gogmagog and Corineus. The name is still preserved in its purity as a designation to the Gogmagog hills in Cambridgeshire. The oldest figure in our Guildhall is supposed to represent Gog-magog, the younger Corineus.

Corineus is one of the principal characters in the tragedy just quoted, and one of the two brothers of Brutus who are companions in his wanderings and his fortunes. He thus narrates his own prowess :

> " When first I followed thee, and thine, brave King
> I hazarded my life and dearest blood,

GOGMAGOG,

THE GIANT IN GUILDHALL.

CORINEUS,

THE GIANT IN GUILDHALL.

To purchase favor at your princely hands,
And for the same in dangerous attempts,
In sundry conflicts, and in divers broils,
I shew'd the courage of my manly mind :
For this I combated with Gathelus,
The brother to Goffarius of Gaul ;
For this I fought with furious Gogmagog,
A savage captain of a savage crew ;
And for these deeds brave Cornwall I receiv'd,
A grateful gift given by a grateful King ;
And for this gift, this life and dearest blood
Will Corineus spend for Brutus' sake."

Now as every national hero in the old time was popularly endowed with gigantic stature, these figures appear to represent the conqueror and the conquered. Their dress, too, would seem to warrant this supposition ; as Gogmagog is armed in accordance with the old tale, while Corineus is habited after the Roman mode, as conventionally depicted at the time of their manufacture.

In the middle of the last century the Guildhall was occupied by shopkeepers,

after the fashion of our bazaars, and one
Thomas Boreman, bookseller, " near the
Giants in Guildhall," published in 1741 two
very small volumes of their " Gigantick
History,"* in which he tells us that as
" Corineus and Gogmagog were two brave
giants, who nicely valued their honor, and
exerted their whole strength and force in
defence of their liberty and country ; so the
City of London, by placing these their
representatives in their Guildhall, emble-

* *The Gigantick History of the two famous Giants
in Guildhall.* Third edition, corrected; printed for
Thomas Boreman, bookseller, near the Giants in Guildhall; and at the Boot and Crown, on Ludgate Hill, 1741.
2 vols. 64mo. For an inspection of these curious volumes
I am indebted to J. Gough Nichols, Esq., F.S.A. Each
volume measures 2½ inches high, by 1½ broad ; a full
page contains fourteen lines and sixty words. These tiny
volumes are bound in boards, covered with the old Dutch
paper, having a green raised pattern on a gold ground.
The price of each volume is marked on the title—the
moderate sum of fourpence!

matically declare, that they will, like mighty giants, defend the honor of their country, and liberties of this their city, which excels all others, as much as those huge giants exceed in stature the common bulk of mankind."

The author of this little volume thus gives his version of the tale of the encounter "wherein the giants were all destroyed, save Goemagog, the hugest among them, who, being in height twelve cubits, was reserved alive, that Corineus might try his strength with him in single combat. Corineus desired nothing more than such a match; but the old giant in a wrestle caught him aloft, and broke three of his ribs. Upon this, Corineus, being desperately enraged, collected all his strength, heaved up Goemagog by main force, and bearing him on his shoulders to the next high rock,

threw him headlong, all shattered, into the
sea, and left his name on the cliff, which
has been ever since called Lan-Goemagog,
that is to say, the Giant's Leap. Thus
perished Goemagog, commonly called Gogmagog, the last of the giants."*

The early popularity of this tale is testi-
fied by its occurrence in the curious history
of the Fitz-Warines,† composed in the
thirteenth century, in Anglo-Norman, no
doubt by a writer who resided on the
Welsh border, and who, in describing a

* I quote from Hone's Extracts, in his article on the
Guildhall Giants, appended to his *Ancient Mysteries
Described*, 8vo, 1823. The book is so rare that he says,
" the copy I consult is the only one I ever saw." To
Hone the merit is due of first drawing attention to the
history of the Civic Giants, and establishing the date
of their fabrication.

† *The History of Fulke Fitz-Warine, an outlawed
Baron in the reign of King John.* Edited from a manu-
script in the British Museum by T. Wright, Esq., for
the Warton Club, 1855.

visit paid by William the Conqueror there,
speaks of that sovereign asking the history
of a burnt and ruined town, and an old
Briton thus giving it to him : " None inhabited these parts except very foul people,
great giants, whose king was called Geomagog.   These heard of the arrival of
Brutus, and went out to encounter him,
and at last all the giants were killed except Geomagog."   He goes on to relate
his death in the encounter with Corineus,
as previously narrated here.   He adds to
the wondrous tale by relating what happened after his death.   " A spirit of the
devil now entered into the body of Geomagog, and came into these parts, and held
possession of the country long, that never
Briton dared to inhabit it.   And long afterwards, King Bran, the son of Donwal, caused
the city to be rebuilt, repaired the walls,

and strengthened the great fosses, and he
made Burgh and Great March.   And the
devil came by night and took away every
thing that was therein, since which tim.
nobody has ever inhabited there."   Payn
Peverel, a " proud and courageous knight,"
listens to the story, and determines to
brave the demon, who comes in a fearful
storm " in the semblance of Geomagog, and
he carried a great club in his hand, and
from his mouth cast fire and smoke, with
which the whole town was illuminated."
He is, however, vanquished by the sign of
the cross, and the sword of the knight,
and discloses the history of the treasures
of the town, promising Payn that he shall
be lord of the soil.   Such was history in
the middle ages.

Those who are curious in tracing the
origin of popular tales, and who agree with

Warton, the historian of our English poetry, in assigning to the Eastern nations the invention of our fabulous lore, may be interested in knowing that "the books of the Arabians and Persians abound with extravagant fictions about the giants Gog and Magog. These they call Jajiouge and Majiouge, and they call the land of Tartary by their names. The Caucasian wall, said to be built by Alexander the Great (though probably formed at an earlier period), from the Caspian to the Black Sea, in order to cover the frontiers of his dominions, and to prevent the incursions of the Scythians, is called by the Orientals the wall of Gog and Magog. This wall, some few fragments of which remain, they pretend to have been built with all sorts of metals. It was a common tradition among the Tartars, that the people of Jajiouge and Majiouge

were perpetually attempting to make a pas-
sage through this fortress; but that they
would not succeed in their attempt till the
day of judgment. About the year 808, the
Caliph Al Amin, having heard wonderful
reports concerning this wall or barrier, sent
his interpreter Salam with a guard of fifty
men to view it. After a dangerous journey
of near two months, Salam and his party
arrived in a desolated country, where they
beheld the ruins of many cities destroyed
by the people of Jajiouge and Majiouge.
In six days more they reached the Castle,
near the mountain Kokaiya, or Caucasus.
This mountain is inaccessibly steep, perpetually covered with snow and thick clouds,
and encompasses the country of Jajiouge
and Majiouge, which is full of cultivated
fields and cities. At the opening of this
mountain the fortress appears; and travel-

ling forward, at the distance of two stages,
they found another mountain, with a ditch
cut through it 150 cubits wide; and, within
the aperture, an iron gate fifty cubits high,
supported by vast buttresses, having an iron
bulwark crowned with iron turrets reaching
to the summit of the mountain itself, which
is too high to be seen. The Governor of
the Castle above-mentioned, once in every
week, mounted on horseback, with ten more,
comes to this gate, and striking it three
times with a hammer weighing five pounds,
hears a murmuring noise from within, supposed to proceed from the Jajiouge and
Majiouge confined there. Salam was told
that they often appeared on the battlements
of the bulwark. Czar Peter I., in his ex-
pedition into Persia, had the curiosity to
survey the ruins of this wall, and some
leagues within the mountains he found a

skirt of it which seemed entire and was about fifteen feet high. It seems at first sight to be built of stone : but it consists of petrified earth, sand, and shells, which compose a substance of great solidity. It has been chiefly destroyed by the neighbouring inhabitants for the sake of the materials, and most of the adjacent towns and villages are built out of its ruins."*

This writer goes on to observe: " How these tremendous heroes got footing in Britain is not hard to discover; for the Arabians having imparted their taste for marvellous and romantic fiction into Europe, by means of the settlement of the Moors in Spain, these were personages of too much importance for the British and Armorican bards to

* *Varieties of Literature :* being principally selections from the Portfolio of the late John Brady, Esq., author of *Clavis Calendaria.* 8vo. 1826.

suffer them to remain behind." Weber, in
the introduction to his *Metrical Romances*,
has the following sensible remarks on this
point: "The Giants of the Odyssey, and
those of Turpin's Chronicle, of Sir Bevis,
and of the Teutonic romances; the Pygmies
of Pliny, and those of the Scandinavians
and Germans; the dragons of Medea, and
those of romance; the enchantments of
Calypso, Medea, Circe, Alcina, and Armida;
in short, the occurrence of fairies, monsters,
and wonders of all kinds in the poetry of
every nation, renders their derivation from
any one particular source, not only very
uncertain, but almost preposterous. They
undoubtedly came originally from Asia, the
cradle of mankind; but all nations in every
age manifestly had a strong inclination to
receive from their neighbours any popular
and successful fiction which obtained among

them, and to communicate their own to them in return."

The famous old traveller, Sir John Maundeville (who performed his journey to the East, between 1322 and 1356), has told his version of the Arabian tale in these words : " In that same regioun ben the mountaynes of Caspye, that men clepen Uber in the contree. Betwene the mountaynes the Jewes of 10 lynages ben enclosed, that men clepen Gothe and Magothe : and they mowe not gon out on no syde. There weren enclosed 22 kynges, with hire peple, that dwelleden betwene the mountaynes of Sythe. There King Alisandre chacede hem betwene the mountaynes ; and there he thought for to enclose hem thorghe werk of his men. But when he saughe that he might not don it, ne bringe it to an ende, he preyed to God of Nature, that he wolde parforme that that he had begonne. And all were it so, that he was a Payneme, and not worthi to ben herd, zit God of his grace closed the mountaynes to gydre : so that thei dwellen there, alle fast ylokked and enclosed with highe mountaynes all aboute, saf only on o syde; and on that syde is the See of Caspye."

When the old Lord Mayor's shows consisted of a series of pageants, invented by poets of no mean fame, the Civic Giants were part of the great public display. On occasions of Royal progresses through the City, they kept "watch and ward" at its gates. In 1415, when the victorious Henry V. made his triumphant entry to London from Southwark, a male and female giant stood at the entrance of London Bridge; the male bearing an axe in his right hand, and in his left the keys of the City hanging to a staff,

as if he had been the porter. In 1432, when
Henry VI. entered London the same way,
"a mighty giant" awaited him, as his champion, at the same place, with a drawn sword,
and an inscription by his side, beginning—

> "All those that be enemies to the King
> I shall them clothe with confusion," &c.

In 1554, when Philip and Mary made their
public entry into London, "two images,
representing two giants, the one named
Corineus and the other Gogmagog, holding
between them certain Latin verses," were
exhibited on London Bridge; "at the draw-
bridge," as Fox informs us in his *Acts and
Monuments*, who speaks of it all as "a great
vaine spectacle," excusing himself for record-
ing the verses, "which, for the vaine osten-
tation of flattery, I overpasse." When
Queen Elizabeth passed through the City,

the day before her coronation, January 12, 1558, great preparations were made to grace the progress with emblematic pageantry. "The final exhibition was at Temple Bar, which was 'finely dressed' with the two giants Gotmagot the Albion, and Corineus the Britain, who held between them a poetic recapitulation of the Pageantries, both in Latin and English."*

When Anthony Munday devised the pageants for the Mayoralty of Sir Leonard Holliday, in 1605, he introduced the whole story of Brutus and his subjugation of Britain in one of them; and " for the more grace and beauty of the show," as he tells us, these two huge giants (whom he names Corineus, and Gogmagog) were fettered by chains of

* Nichol's *Progresses of Queen Elizabeth;* and *Accounts of Royal Processions in the City of London.* 8vo. 1831,

gold to the Mount upon which Brutus and
the other characters were placed. Mars-
ton, in his play of the *Dutch Courtezan*,
1605, speaks of " the giants stilts that
stalk before my Lord Mayor's pageants;"
and giants formed part of the great shows
made on the setting of the City watch
on Midsummer eve.   In 1672, when
Thomas Jordan, the City Poet, composed
the pageant for Sir Robert Hanson,
Mayor, he says : " I must not omit to tell
you, that marching in the van of these five
pageants are two exceeding rarities to be
taken notice of, that is, there are two extreme
great giants, each of them at least fifteen
foot high, that do sit, and are drawn by
horses in two several chariots, moving,
talking, and taking tobacco as they ride
along, to the great admiration and delight of
all the spectators.   At the conclusion·of the

show, they are to be set up in Guildhall,
where they may be daily seen all the year,
and I hope never to be demolished by such
dismal violence as happened to their predecessors." This " dismal violence" was the
Great Fire of London, by which the Hall
was gutted, but not destroyed. Hatton, in
his *New View of London*, 1708, says it was
"extremely well beautified and repaired, both
in and outside, in 1669, and two new figures
of gigantic magnitude will be as before."
These new figures are the present ones,
which succeeded those described as carried
through the streets by Jordan. The history
of the change is thus given in the little book
published in Guildhall, 1741, and already
alluded to, " Before the present giants inhabited Guildhall, there were two giants
made only of wicker work and pasteboard,
put together with great art and ingenuity;

and these two terrible original giants had
the honor yearly to grace my Lord Mayor's
show, being carried in great triumph in the
time of the pageants; and when that
eminent annual service was over, remounted
their old stations in Guildhall, till by reason
of their very great age, old time, with the
help of a number of city rats and mice, had
eaten up all their entrails. The dissolution
of the two old, weak, and feeble giants, gave
birth to the two present substantial and
majestic giants ; who, by order, and at the
City charge, were formed and fashioned.
Captain Richard Saunders, an eminent
carver in King Street, Cheapside, was their
father ; who, after he had completely finished,
clothed, and armed these his two sons, they
were immediately advanced to their lofty
stations in Guildhall, which they have peaceably enjoyed ever since the year 1708."

This incidental notice of "their father" enabled Hone to make researches among the City accounts at the Chamberlain's office, and under the head of "Extraordinary Works" for 1707, he fortunately discovered among the sums "paid for repairing of the Guildhall and Chappell," an entry in the following words:

"To *Richard Saunders*, Carver, Seaventy Pounds,
by order of the Co'mittee, for repairing
Guildhall, dated y⁰ xth of April, 1707,
for work by him done . . . . £70"

"This entry of the payment," says Hone, "confirms the relation of the gigantic historian. Saunders's bill, which doubtless contained the charges for the two giants, and all the vouchers before 1786, belonging to the Chamberlain's office, were destroyed by a fire in that year." Saunders's Captaincy was in that valuable, but much-ridiculed force, the City Train-band.

D

The "lofty stations" mentioned as awarded to these figures in the Guildhall, was not their present locality; they were originally placed on each side the entrance to the Council chamber, and were removed to the window where they now stand in 1815, when Hone thoroughly examined them, and found them to be ponderously constructed of wood, but hollow within; they are upwards of fourteen feet in height, and were evidently made for the permanent decoration of the building, and not for carrying through the City on festive days, as were their predecessors.

Notices of the earlier giants, popular favourites though they were, are few and incidental in the literature of the day. They are supposed by Brand (in his *Popular Antiquities*) to be alluded to, when in their original position at the gates of Guild-

hall (as noted p. 11), by Bishop Hall in his
Satires (Book vi., Sat. 1), where, speaking
of an angry poet, he says that he—

> " ———— makes such faces, that me seemes I see
> Some foul Megæra in the Tragedie,
> Threat'ning her twined snakes at Tantale's ghost;
> Or the grim visage of some frowning post,
> The crab-tree porter of the Guildhall gates,
> When he his frightful beetle elevates."

In Shirley's *Contention for Honour and
Riches*, 1633 (and afterwards in his *Honoria
and Mammon*, 1652), he ridicules the annual Civic Pageants on Lord Mayor's Day,
and the citizens' love of good cheer after
them: "You march to Guildhall, with
every man his spoon in his pocket, where
you look upon the giants, and feed like
Saracens."

Bishop Corbet, who died 1635, in his
Iter Boreale, written about the middle of
James the First's reign, alludes to them,

when speaking of those at Holmby, the seat of Sir Christopher Hatton, the " Dancing Chancellor " of Queen Elizabeth :

> " Oh you, that do Guildhall and Holmeby keep
> Soe carefully, when both their founders sleepe,
> You are good giants."

In the *British Bibliographer*, vol. 4, p. 277, the following verses are quoted from a broadside printed in 1660; and afterwards by Archdeacon Nares, in his *Glossary* :

> " And such stout Coronæus was, from whom
> Cornwall's first honor, and her name doth come.
> For though he sheweth not so great, nor tall,
> In his dimensions set forth at Guildhall,
> Know 'tis a poet only can define
> A gyant's posture in a gyant's line.
>   *   *   *   *
> And thus attended by his direful dog
> The gyant was (God bless us !) Gogmagog."

George Wither, in his *Joco-Serio: Strange*

Newes of a Discourse between two Dead Giants, 1661, alludes to them by different names:

> " Big-bon'd Colbrant, and great Brandamore,
> The giants in Guildhall   .   .   .   .
> Where they have had a place to them assign'd
> At publick meetings, now time out of mind."

This brief poem " was composed by occasion of a scurrilous pamphlet, entitled, *A Dialogue between Brandamore and Colbrant, the two Giants in Guildhall,*" in which Wither was alluded to in no flattering terms. His poem contains no other notice of them; and the names, which he had evidently borrowed from his adversary, seem to have been the capricious invention of that unknown satirist, as they are not met with elsewhere.

In the Latin poem, *Londini quod re-*

liquum, 1667, quoted by Brand, in his *Popular Antiquities*, they are thus noticed:

> " Haud procul, excelsis olim prætoria pinnis
>   Surgebant pario marmore fulsit opus.
> Alta *duo Ætnei* servabant atria *fratres*.
>   Prætextaque frequeus splenduit aula toga.
> Hic populo Augustus reddebat jura senatus,
>   Et sua prætori sella curulis erat.
> Sed neque Vulcanum juris reverentia cepit,
>   Tuta satellitio nec fuit aulo suo.
> Vidi, et exurgas, dixit, speciosior aula
>   Atque frequens solita curia lite strepat."

Among the fireworks upon the Thames, at the coronation of James II. and his Queen, April 24, 1685, the giants appeared; the City of London having contributed part of the expenses. The narrative of the proceedings by R. Lowman, 1685,* describes

---

* Quoted from the folio half-sheet by Hone. Sandford, in his account of these festivities, takes no note of these figures, nor are they represented in his engraving of the fireworks, which otherwise accords with the above description.

a raft erected in the middle of the river, having on it two pyramids, between them a brass sun, and a cross and crown, in fire-works; in front "were placed the statues of the two giants of Guildhall, in lively colours and proportions facing Whitehall, the backs of which were all filled with fiery materials, and from the first deluge of fire till the end of the sport, which lasted near an hour, the two giants, the cross, and the sun, grew all in a light flame in the figures described, and burned without abatement of matter."

Ned Ward, in his *London Spy*, 1699, describes a visit to Guildhall, "which we entered with as great astonishment to see the giants, as the Morocco Ambassador did London when he saw the snow fall. I asked my friend the meaning and design of setting up these two lubberly preposterous figures;

for I suppose they had some peculiar end
in it. 'Truly,' says my friend, 'I am
wholly ignorant of what they intended by
them, unless they were set up to show the
City what huge loobies their forefathers
were, or else to fright stubborn apprentices
into obedience : for the dread of appearing
before two such monstrous loggerheads, will
sooner reform their manners, or mould them
in compliance with their masters' will, than
carrying them before my Lord Mayor, or
the Chamberlain of London ; for some of
them are as much frighted at the names of
Gog and Magog, as little children are at
the terrible sound of Rawhead and Bloody-
bones." From this we may gather, as Hone
has shrewdly observed, that some representa-
tions of the popular figures garnished the
old hall, after the fire that Hatton alludes
to, and before the construction of the present

ones. It is further confirmed by the title-
page of an 8vo. tract published in 1684,
describing " the gyant, or the miracle of
nature, being that so much admired young
man, born in Ireland, believed to be as big
as one of the gyants in Guildhall." It is
most probable that, according to old custom,
the figures that graced the Mayoralty shows
in 1672 were set up in the hall. Their
popularity is attested in another part of
Ward's book, by the exclamation of a coach-
man: "Pay me my fare, or, by Gog and
Magog, you shall feel the smart of my
whipcord."

Upon the reparation of the hall in 1706,
the present figures were placed in a conspicuous position; but not, as before observed, in their present one. There is a
view of the interior of Guildhall, apparently
engraved about this time (in the *Crowle*

Illustrated Pennant, in the British Museum),
which has a brief description of the scene
beneath it, in which we are told, " over the
steps going into the Mayor's court, at some
height stand giants of monstrous height and
bigness ; the one holding a pole-axe, the
other a halbert." An elaborately constructed
door-case or porch was built over the steps
alluded to, exactly opposite the great gate
of Guildhall. It consisted of a semi-gothic
foundation, upon which imitation palm-
trees were planted, they in turn supported
a balcony, in front of that was placed a clock
in a carved case, surrounded by emblematic
figures of Time, &c. Upon brackets on
each side of this balcony the giants were
stationed, and the first notice of them in
their new position is given in Bragg's *Ob-
server*, Dec. 25, 1706, when narrating the
placing of the colors taken at Ramilies in

the Guildhall : "When I entered the hall,
I protest, masters, I never saw so much
joy in the countenances of the people in my
life, as in the cits on this occasion ; nay, the
very giants stared at the colors with all the
eyes they had, and smiled as well as they
could."*

In *London in Miniature*, 1755, they are
thus briefly alluded to : "In the middle
of the hall on the north side, over the
door leading to the Mayor's court, is a

---

* Their appearance is less favourably noted in a political
satire on a procession to court in the early part of the
eighteenth century, for a redress of grievances; it is said
of the citizens composing it,—

"The giants in Guildhall could not have looked
grimmer."

The famous orator Henley took an opportunity of
ridiculing the annual Lord Mayor's show, and "the
two giants walking out to keep holiday." See an adver-
tisement of this lecture (Oct. 21, 1730) reprinted by
Hone.

very handsome clock and dial, finely gilt
and ornamented, and on each side thereof
are the huge figures of two monstrous
giants, about fourteen feet high, finely
carved in wood, and painted."

In the *New London Spy; or, a Twenty-
four Hours' Ramble through the Bills of
Mortality* (8vo., 1760, p. 71), they are
thus described, after the fashion of Ned
Ward: "The first objects that struck me
were two monstrous figures of immense
bulk, and stupendous height, fixed on each
side of the clock; as if designed to strike
all that entered with astonishment and
awe. As I could by no means devise
the design of placing these preposterous
figures in the most conspicuous part of the
hall, I referred to my sage friend for his
opinion; but he could not resolve me
with any degree of certainty. He conjec-

tured that our forefathers might weakly believe the stories related of giants and their mighty feats, particularly those of the renowned Gog and Magog, which these unwieldy lumps, by some, are supposed to represent."

In Brand's *Popular Antiquities* (Bohn's edition, vol. 1, p. 324), a similarly uncivil notice of them is given from Grosley's *Tour to London*, translated by Nugent, 1772; in which their very existence is attributed to the " Gothic taste " of the English nation.   By far the best account of their appearance, combined with some curious details of the structure they supported, is to be found in Dodsleys' *London and its Environs Described*, 1761, vol. 3, p. 102, as follows: "Nearly fronting the gate, are nine or ten steps, leading to the Lord Mayor's court, over which is a balcony

supported at each end by four iron pillars
in the form of palm trees; by these is a
small enclosure on each side on the top
of the steps, used on some occasions as
offices for clerks to write in, each being
just sufficient to hold one person. Under
these are two prisons called Little Ease,
from the lowness of the ceiling, by which
prisoners were obliged to sit on the floor;
these prisons are intended for city apprentices, who, upon complaint and a strict
examination into the offence, were sometimes committed thither by the Chamberlain,
whose office is at the right hand, at the
head of the steps. In the front of this
balcony is a clock, on the frame of which
is carved the four cardinal virtues, with
the figure of Time on the top, and a
cock on each side of him. But the most
extraordinary figures are yet behind; these

are two monstrous giants, which stand on
the outside of the balcony, close to the
wall, one on each side : they have black
and bushy beards ; one holds an halbert,
and the other a ball set round with spikes,
hanging by a chain to a long staff. These
absurd ornaments, which Mr. Strype sup-
poses were designed to represent an ancient
Briton and a Saxon, are painted, as if to give
them the greater appearance of life, and ren-
der them more formidable to children."

There is a curious print in the *European
Magazine* of 1810, designed to exhibit the
giants only, and showing the upper part of
the balcony and clock ; it is the only in-
stance in which they were honoured by
exclusive delineation, until Hone, in 1823,
still more correctly perpetuated their features
by the aid of the admirable pencil of George
Cruikshank.

Pennant, speaking of Guildhall, merely says: "Facing the entrance are two tremendous figures, by some called Gog and Magog; by Stow, an antient Briton and Saxon. I leave others to determine the important decision." This loose reference to Stow has been pretty constantly repeated, although pregnant with grave error; it would lead to the inference that they were so known and named in the reign of Elizabeth; but the fact is, Stow does not mention them at all: they are thus named by Strype in his edition of Stow's book, as correctly noted by Dodsley; and therefore the names, instead of being authorities of the reign of Elizabeth, end in being conjectures in that of Anne.

The view of the interior of the Guildhall, published by G. Hawkins in 1801, shows both giants bearing pendant spikes on

chains secured to a poleaxe, but it is probably an oversight. The lower range of
lights in the great west window was at
this time blocked up, and Beckford's monument was in the centre: pictures of judges
occupied the sides where the giants now
stand. On this popular monument Pennant
makes an unusually illnatured remark for
him. He says : " The principal figure was
also a giant in his day, the Raw-head
and Bloody-bones to the good folks of St.
James's."

The best view of the locality is in the
fine print published by Boydell (from a
painting by Wm. Miller, engraved by Ben-
jamin Smith), representing the ceremony
of administering the oath of allegiance on
the 8th of November, the day preceding
Lord Mayor's day, to Alderman Newnham,
in 1782. The armed giant, with the shield

E

and halbert, is very clearly shown standing on an ornamental bracket beside the
gallery.

In 1815, when the hall underwent reparation, this doorcase, balcony, and clock
were removed, the giants were repainted
and gilt, and set on pedestals on each side
the great west window, where they now
stand. In 1837, they were again restored;
and in that year, Alderman Lucas being
Mayor, copies of these giants fourteen feet
in height, were introduced in the Lord
Mayor's show: each walked by the aid
of a man within them, and they from
time to time turned their faces to the
spectators who lined the streets. It was
the final exhibition of the olden glories
of that day.

Anciently the giants were frequently paraded before the gratified eyes of the citi-

zens.   Thus we are told in *Machyn's Diary*
(printed by the Camden Society), that in
1553, "the xvij day of Marche, cam through
London from Algatt, Master Maynard, the
Shreyff of London, with a standard and
dromes, and after gyants boyth great and
small."   The citizens appear to have willingly taxed themselves for such monsters,
for May games, Midsummer pageants, &c.
Thus the churchwardens' accounts of St.
Andrew Hubbard parish, in the city of
London, have an entry, A.D. 1533, "Receyved for the Jeyantt, xix$^{d.}$;" and again, in
1535, "Receyved for the Jeyantt, ij · viij$^{d.}$."
Puttenham, in his *Arte of English Poesie*,
1589, speaks of "Midsommer pageants in
London, where, to make the people wonder,
are set forth great and uglie gyants, marching as if they were alive, and armed at all
points, but within they are stuffed full of

brown paper and tow, which the shrewd
boyes, underpeeping, do guilefully discover,
and turne to a great derision." These
" Midsommer pageants " were the annual
settings of the Watch for the protection of
the City, a sight our monarchs thought it
worth a journey to see, and of which Stow
has left so graphic an account, informing
us, " the Mayor had besides his giant three
pageants; each of the sheriffs had besides
their giants but two pageants."* The setting of the Watch at Chester was conducted
on the eve of the festival of St. John the
Baptist, in the same pompous manner; and

* Stow relates in his *Annals*, under date 1510 : " On
Midsummer Eve, at night, King Henry came privily into
West-Cheap, being clothed in one of the coats of his
guard," to see the great show; with which he was
so much gratified, that he afterwards visited the
City in state with his Queen and Nobles, to give
them a share in his " royal pleasure," and patronize
the festivities.

in 1564, it was directed that there should
be annually, according to ancient custom,
a pageant, consisting of four giants, with
animals, hobby-horses, and other figures
therein specified. Hone, who follows Strutt
in this account, continues : " In 1599,
Henry Hardman, Esq., the Mayor of that
year, from religious motives, caused the
giants in the Midsummer show ' to be
broken, and not to goe *the devil in his
feathers.'* " Now, as Hone has repeated
this note elsewhere in his popular works,
it is worth correcting, for he seems to go
wrong when describing Hardman's doings
at Chester. The following extract from
the Corporation Records in the *History of
Chester*, 8vo., 1815, clearly shows that the
" devil in his feathers " was a peculiar
feature in the butchers' display on this
occasion, and that the giants are not alluded

to by such a phrase at all, and were not "broken," but only put aside:

"1599, Henry Hardman, Mayor, caused the giants in the Midsummer show not to go, the devil in his feathers not to ride for the butchers, but a boy as the others, and the cuppes and cannes, and dragon, and naked boy to be put away; but caused a man in complete armour to go before the shows in their stead."*

---

* On this circumstance, Hone says : "One conjecture may be hazarded, that, as after the Mayor of Chester had ordered the giants there to be destroyed, he provided a man in armour as a substitute ; so perhaps the dissolution of the old London giants, and the incapacity of the new ones for the duty of Lord Mayor's show, occasioned the appearance of the men in armour in that procession." The author of the tiny "Gigantick History" already quoted, shows that the armed man was the Civic Champion at the Mayor's feast, in imitation of the King's Champion at Royal Coronations, a semi-regal state being always held in Guildhall at the inauguration of a Mayor. He thus describes the custom more than a century since : "About twelve-a-clock this mighty champion mounted

From "the Banes [or Proclamations]
which are read before the beginning of the
Plays of Chester,"* we again learn that
this devil was peculiar to the Butchers' Company, who always played the "Temptation
of Christ," in which he appears to have been
so popular a character, as to have been

on his horse (in complete armour from the Tower), with
a great drawn sword in his hand, advances at the head
of the Worshipful Company of Armourers, who set out
from their hall in Coleman Street, and proceed to a large
house near Trig stairs, belonging to that Company ;
where having regaled themselves, they set out again,
going thro' St. Paul's Churchyard, Ludgate, and so on to
Salisbury Court, in Fleet Street ; where having showed
themselves, they return back, and march before my
Lord's company through the City to King Street, and
then to their own hall in Coleman Street : and after this
bold Champion hath seen the Worshipful Company safe
housed, he dismounts his prancer, and so concludes the
ceremony." The significance of the one champion, has
therefore been lost in the vulgar taste for many "men
in armour" in the procession.

* Wright's edition of the *Chester Mysteries*, published
by the Shakespeare Society, 1843.

paraded a little too proudly at other times. The Company is thus addressed:

" ————you, bowchers of this citie,
The storie of Sathan, that Christe woulde needes tempte,
Set out as accoostomablie have yee,
The devill in his fethers all ragged and rente."

Now, as it was usual (particularly in the fifteenth century) to represent the angels entirely covered with feathers; as may be seen in many examples, but in none better than the painted glass in New College Chapel, Oxford ;* and Lucifer was " a fallen angel," he was properly habited in feathers, but possibly made grotesque and horrible, by being black and ragged. That the other parts of this show were not long discontinued appears by Strutt's account in the Introduc-

* Engraved in *The Calendar of the Anglican Church.
Illustrated*, published by Parker of Oxford, 1851. They were put up before 1386, when the building was completed.

tion to his *Sports and Pastimes*, which we now quote:

"In the year 1601, John Ratclyffe, beer-brewer, being Mayor, ' sett out the giaunts and Midsommer show, as of oulde it was wont to be kept.' In the time of the Common-wealth this spectacle was discontinued, and the giants, with the beasts, were destroyed. At the restoration of Charles II. it was agreed by the citizens to replace the pageant as usual, on the eve of the festival of St. John the Baptist, in 1661; and as the following computation of the charges for the different parts of the show are exceed-ingly curious, I shall lay them before the reader without any farther apology. We are told that ' all things were to be made new, by reason the ould modells were all broken.' The computist then proceeds: 'For finding all the materials, with the

workmanship of the four great giants, all to
be made new, as neere as may be lyke as
they were before, at five pounds a giant the
least that can be, and four men to carry
them at two shillings and sixpence each.'
The materials for the composition of these
monsters are afterwards specified to be
'hoops of various magnitudes, and other
productions of the cooper, deal boards, nails,
pasteboard, scaleboard, paper of various
sorts, with buckram, size cloth, and old
sheets for their bodies, sleeves, and skirts,
which were to be coloured.' One pair of the
'olde sheets' were provided to cover the
'father and mother giants.' Another article
specifies 'three yards of buckram for the
mother's and daughter's hoods;" which
seems to prove that three of these stupendous pasteboard personages were the representatives of females. There were 'also

tinsille, tinfoil, gold and silver leaf, and
colours of different kinds, with glue and
paste in abundance.'   Respecting the last
article a very ridiculous entry occurs in the
bill of charges, it runs thus :   ' For arsnick
to put into the paste to save the giants from
being eaten by the rats, one shilling and
fourpence.'"

Chester and Coventry were the two grand
cities for public displays in the olden time.
Sharp, in his *Dissertation on the Pageants
or Dramatic Mysteries anciently performed
at Coventry, by the trading Companies of
that City* (Coventry, 1825), has furnished
very curious details of the giants displayed
by the Capper's Company, from 1533 to
1560, as preserved in their account books.
The first entry, in 1533, is " payed for the
Gyant, xxvij^s. viij^d.;" in the next year we
have "paid for dressyng the gyant vi^d.;"

while charges continue during those years
for dressing, mending, and painting him;
as well as sums for "beryng the giants
about the streets, which appears to have
been at the rate of one shilling per night.
In 1547, is an entry of ninepence, for
canvass to make the giant a new skirt;
again in 1553, are others for " mendyng and
payntyng the Gyand;" which, as they are
the last, would seem to infer that twenty
years' wear and tear had thoroughly under-
mined his constitution. The most curious
item is that of twopence "paid for the
candlestick in his head, and the light:"
which charge for " waxe candell" is more
than once repeated; showing that it was the
custom to light the head at night, the
ceremony of setting the Midsummer Watch
always taking place after dark.

By the Drapers' accounts of Coventry, we

find that they owned two giants. In 1556, they have a charge of twenty shillings, "payd to Robert Crowe for makyng of the gyanes," and in the same year they pay two men eleven-pence each for carrying them. By an entry of 2s. 6d. paid for painting the giant's wife, we learn that these figures were male and female, as many still are in some continental cities; and, like them, they swelled public shows by the loan of their figures, for in 1557, there is an entry in their books of the receipt of 2s. 4d. "for the hyar of the giant's wife at Midsummer."

Other places followed the example. Dr. Plot, in his *History of Oxfordshire*, speaks of the custom of keeping Midsummer Eve "in great jollity" at Burford, and of carrying "up and down the town" a dragon and a giant; and Sharp, in the work just quoted, tells us, that in 1814 "he saw at

Salisbury a figure of a man, ten or twelve
feet high, belonging to the Taylors' Company,
and called St. Christopher (by the common
people termed *the giant*). This was exhibited in the various streets, attended by
two men grotesquely habited, bearing his
sword and club; a drum and fife played
tunes, to which the figure was made to
dance in a solemn unwieldy manner, by a
man concealed within, and perfectly hidden
by its long drapery. The attendants danced
around the giant, watching carefully to check
by the sword or club, any deviation from a
perpendicular position."

It is now about fifteen years since the
author of this little volume visited the hall
of the Tailors' Company at Salisbury, and
saw in that neglected building their once-
popular giant mouldering to decay. The
frontispiece to this volume has been copied

from the sketch he then made of the figure.
Its substructure was a framework of lath
and hoop, similar to that used for " Jack-in-
the-Green " on May-day, and allowed a
person to walk inside and carry the figure,
he being fully concealed by the drapery,
which was of coloured chintz, bordered
with red and purple, and trimmed with
yellow fringe. The head was modelled in
paste-board, and coloured, the hair being
formed of tow; a gold-laced cocked hat and
yellow cockade completed the costume. A
large wooden pipe was stuck in the mouth,
after the fashion of the London giants of
1672; a branch of artificial laurel was
placed in the right hand. The club and
sword were both carved in wood, and painted.
This was the last of the old perambulating
English giants, and the only one whose
figure has been delineated.

I trace all these English giants to the much
older Guild observances of the continental
cities. We owe to the merchantmen of the
Low Countries that determination to carry
out great trading enterprises through impedi-
ments of which we now can form very slight
ideas; and which resulted in the overthrow of
the feudal system, the establishment of commerce on a firm basis, and the rise and
prosperity of great cities with a free trade;
such as Antwerp was, and London is.
Their prosperous traders rivalled the glories
of the old nobility in the palaces they
constructed for their Guildhalls; and
having no pride of ancestry, they chose
the legends of their old cities for display
on public occasions. Hence they typified
the legendary history of Antwerp in the
giant Antigonus; that of Lyderic, the
Forester of Flanders; of the gigantic horse

Bayard, upon which ride the four sons of Aymon; of Goliath, the giant of Ath; and the family of giants of Malines, Brussels, and Douai. Gayant, the giant of Douai, is twenty-two feet in height; and with his spear touches the house tops of the old city. On solemn occasions of great popular observance, such as the entries of Sovereigns into cities; or in great religious centenary solemnities, like the feasts of St. Rombaud at Malines, or St. Macaire at Mons, there is a reunion of giants. They are lent by the corporations of each town to swell the public shows. The only giant who has not visited his friends is he of Antwerp: the reason being that there is no gate in the city large enough for him to go through. In the old time it was necessary to lower the lanthorns, and remove the chains or ropes by which they were

F

suspended, in all streets through which the figure passed. It always occupied a part in processions to honour kings and potentates, when it was made to promenade the city. On the entry of Philip, Prince of Spain (afterwards Philip II.), the burghers bestowed large sums on a grand public spectacle, and the giant was exhibited, seated in a Doric temple, in the great square opposite the Town-hall. Above him, upon the abacus, was this inscription :

ILLE EGO (QUEM FAMA EST, HIS OLIM LOCIS NOVAM EXERCVISSE TYRANNIDEM) ET SI COR-PORIS VASTITATE ADHVCDVM SIM FORMIDABILIS, POSITA JAM FERITATE, TIBI PHILIPPE PRINCEPS MAX. LIBENS CEDO, TVAEQVE ME POTESTATI VLTRO SVBIICIO.

Grapheus, secretary to the city of Antwerp, in his descriptive quarto volume of the festivities then given, has published an engraving of this figure ; and its history in the following words :

" There is a very popular tradition (which
we ourselves, as boys, have helped to sus-
tain) that this giant, called Antigonus, inhabited the locality on the river Scheldt,
where, at the present day, may be seen the
ruins of the castle of old Antwerp, with the
walls partly destroyed, the reputed pre-
torium, the public prison, and the temple
of Saint Valburg, which (they say) was
formerly sacred to Mars.*

" This Antigonus, relying upon his im-
pregnable castle, began to play the tyrant;
to exact a toll from travellers who passed
that way; and to exercise a cruel rule over
the neighbourhood. If those whom he
caught did not pay the impost levied, or
refused to pay, he extorted it by violence;

* Verbyst, in his account of Antwerp, 1646, tells us
that this castle (probably a Roman ruin) stood on the
site of the house of the Knights Crusaders of the
Teutonic Order, within the borcht or bailywick.

and those who could not pay in money, he did not allow to depart without cutting off one of their hands. From this circumstance the inhabitants called the place *Hantworp*—that is, hand tossing*—which word (the aspirate being dropt, and the *o* being changed into *e*), we pronounce *Antwerp*. We find in ancient writings it was sometimes called *Andoverp*, as well as *Antorp*, and *Antorff*.†

"But there was at this time a prince of the province called Brabon (from whom Brabant is named, as some suppose), who, resolving to put an end to the insolent tyranny of the giant, boldly attacked him,

---

* In the original Latin, a word, *manujactionem*, has been coined to express this *hand throwing* or *hand tossing*.

† The most probable derivation of the name is from *an t'Werf*, the city *on the Wharf* or quay.—*De Wez, Dict. Geog. des Pays-Bas.*

and with heroic valour encountered, over-
threw, and slew him; thus liberating the
country.

"There are various versions of this
legend, as is consistent with the rude age
in which it originated: they are not, however, less worthy of credit than the stories
of the ancients about their gods, such as
Jupiter, Juno, Saturn, and Mercury.*

"Respecting the cutting off the hands,
it is vouched for by many trustworthy
persons of this city, whom we ourselves
were acquainted with, and who are alive
at this day, that they themselves have
seen exhumed, on the occasion of the
excavation of the foundations of some old

* One version of the legend affirms that Antigonus
had a retreat under the Scheldt, but that the means of
access to it are now unknown; but if it could be discovered, the giant's chair of massive gold would reward
the explorer.

buildings, certain small coffers* full of flesh-
less men's hands that had been cut off.

"Moreover, there may be still seen in our
senate. house some perfect bones of unusual size, with iron chains hanging to
them, which are universally ascribed to
the giant himself. To whomsoever they
may have belonged, skilful anatomists
assert they are the bones of a man of
extraordinary stature. They are the hip-
bone, a tooth, the arm, the shoulder-blade,
and the tibia. From the measurement
of the bones it is calculated that the man
to whom they belonged measured eighteen
feet in height.†

---

* It is probable that these coffers were Roman fune-
real vases, containing fragments of bone, the result of
cremation.

† The artist Albert Durer mentions in his *Journal of
Travels in the Netherlands*, 1520 and 1521, having seen
at Antwerp, in the former year, " the bones of a giant

"We recollect that these bones were the subject of some Latin epigrams which are now preserved in the house of the keeper of the public treasury. They are as follows :

ON THE HIP-BONE.

Tanta hæc horrifici fuerit si coxa gigantis,
　　Cætera quanta illi membra fuisse putes?

THE TOOTH.

Faucibus immensis dens hic stetit, ore voraci
　　Quivisset solidos ille vorare boves.

THE ARM.

Quam fuerit forti munitus robore, sævus
　　Ille vir, id cubiti pars monet ista sui.

THE SHOULDER-BLADE.

Ardua terribilis spatula hæc est (crede) tyranni,
　　Quid reris quantum sustinuisset onus?

THE TIBIA.

Gestavit vastum vasta ist hæc tibia corpus,
　　Enceladum æquavit, non dubium, ille gradu."

Such is the earliest account (published in

who had been eighteen feet high." They were most probably fossil bones of extinct animals.—See what is said on this subject in the note, p. 4.

1550) of this celebrated figure, from the official pen of an officer of the city of Antwerp. The tale is further commemorated by a figure surmounting the iron-work canopy of the famous well opposite the great west door of the cathedral; the work of the artist Quintyn Matsys while he was a blacksmith. It represents Antigonus, fully armed, bearing a sword in one hand, and with the other throwing away the severed hand of one of his victims. But an equally curious adaptation of the old story appears to this day in the arms of Antwerp (see cut in title page of this book, from a design by Rubens, used in the festivities noted p. 76), a castle of three towers *argent*, surmounted by two hands, *gules*, one dexter, the other sinister. The castle being that of the giant, the hands those of his opponents.

Verbyst, speaking of the old legend, in

1646, says, that the citizens " appeal to
the two most solemn annual processions
which take place at Antwerp, on the ani-
versaries of the circumcision, and of the
assumption of the Virgin, when from time
immemorial it has been the custom to
carry in procession a colossal statue of
the giant, followed by a number of persons
who appear to have had their hands cut off."

In the woodcut executed by John Jeghers,
about 1640, delineating the principal pageants in these great popular shows, the
giant is preceded by two men in the livery
of the city, carrying the severed hands as
a trophy. He is attended by six smaller
giants, one playing a pipe and another a
tabor. In the show of 1685, there were
eight of these giants, some dressed in the
costume of Spain and the Netherlands, and
others in French, Dutch, and English

fashions; and these all danced round the
great giant, " to denote that Antwerp,
symbolized by him, was at peace with
all nations."

This famous figure, which still exists, was
designed in 1534 by Peter Van Aelst, painter
to the Emperor Charles the Fifth, and constructed under his superintendence.   A
native writer says: "It has been admired
by all lovers of art as one of its greatest
wonders, by reason of its great size, and
the exceeding cleverness with which it is
constructed." The figure is nearly forty
feet in height: like our Guildhall giants,
it is carved in wood, coloured, and gilt,
but hollow throughout; and is borne about
the streets in a car drawn by eight strong
horses.

In the noble illustrated volumes which
issued from the presses of this old city,

ANTIGONUS,

THE GIANT OF ANTWERP.

74b

and recorded the sumptuous pageants with which its merchant-princes delighted to receive royal visitors, are many fine engravings of the giant. In that descriptive of the entry of Francis, Duke of Brabant and Anjou, 1582, Antigonus appears with the French flag at the end of his truncheon, in compliment to the Duke, who was further flattered in some Latin verses appended to his car; " the giant turned his head (by an artifice) towards his highness, and holding in his hand the arms of Spain, let them fall, leaving those of Anjou,"—a delicate compliment to the late and former rulers, who both helped to ruin the old city. In the description by Bochius of the spectacles on the advent of Ernest, Archduke of Austria, 1595, the giant, he says, was stationed in front of the Town-hall, with war, discord, and envy

conquered at his feet,—a political illu-
sion to the times. Under the benign
influence of Albert and Isabella, the Ant-
werpians exhibited on the occasion of
their public entry in 1602, the giant
disarmed by cupids, who were perched on
various parts of the figure, as if in the
act of relieving him of his military
equipment. When Ferdinand of Austria
made his triumphal entry as Governor of Belgium in 1635, the giant
was stationed in his old situation near
the Town-hall.* The very best engrav-

* In Gevartius' magnificent volume, devoted to a description of the festivities, the figure may be recognised
in the general plan of Antwerp. On this occasion Rubens
invented and superintended the pageantry, for which the
genius of the great Fleming was peculiarly suited. His
original designs are still preserved in the gallery at Antwerp. It may be worth remarking, that the city is always
personified as a female crowned with a castle, above
which are the severed hands.

ing of this figure, is the large folio
print published in 1665 by Wm. Hendricx,
and from which our cut is copied.

In the *Magazin de la Ville*, Rue Bellard,
this enormous figure is stored with equally
unwieldly companions. The building is
nearly as large as our Guildhall; vast
folding doors reaching from ground to roof
give admittance and exit to the pageants,
which are still paraded through the streets
on great occasions, and were all exhibited
when her Majesty Queen Victoria visited
Antwerp in September, 1843. They consist
of emblematic figures, a ship fully rigged,
a gigantic whale, &c. Three years ago,
while staying in Antwerp, the author
obtained permission from the municipal
authorities to examine these figures at
leisure. It was a singular sight, this
great hall crowded with these vast figures;

something like a visit to Brobdignag. Chief among them sat Antigonus; a door in the pedestal or seat on which he reposes allows access to a stair, by which you may ascend the body, the staircase continuing to the shoulders, where a platform is constructed, in the centre of which is a winch, used to move the giant's head backward and forward as he goes along, by a man who stands on this platform during his progress; the neck being made to move freely in the gorget which surrounds the breastplate.

Having bestowed so much space in the consideration of this, the most popular and curious of the Continental family of giants, we may now more briefly allude to some others, which belong to other old cities; the most remarkable being the giant of Douai, whose history has been

78a

GAYANT AND HIS FAMILY,

THE GIANTS OF DOUAI.

told by Monsieur le Conseiller Quenson
in an octavo volume published at Douai
in 1839.

Gayant, the giant of Douai, and his
family, are represented in our cut as they
are seen on the fête-days of July;* and
consist of the giant himself, (who was also
sometimes termed *Jehan Gélon*); his spouse,
named *Marie Cagenon*; a young male giant,
his son, called *M. Jacquot;* a young giantess,
his daughter, termed *Mademoiselle Filion;*
and a young infant, called *Binbin, ce tiot
tourni,*—" a surname of affection given
him by the people by reason of his age, and
his eyes badly turned," says M. Quenson.
The giant is twenty-two feet in height, in
the costume of a warrior of the time of the

* The size of our page will not admit the full height
of the tilting-spear the giant carries, which is nearly as
tall as himself; and is decorated with a streamer or
pennon at its point.

renaissance, with a helmet, breastplate, thigh-pieces, and apron of chain-mail, from which descends a huge petticoat, reaching to the ground, and serving to conceal the nine men who move the figure within.* The giantess, his wife, is two feet shorter than her lord, and is elaborately dressed in the costume of the time of *François Premier*, decorated with enormous jewels, and bearing in one hand a feather-fan. Her eldest son, only twelve feet in height, is in the full court dress of the sixteenth century; her daughter ("of delicate complexion, and light hair") is two feet less than her brother; the infant being only eight feet high, is habited in a child's loose dress, with the national *bourrelet* or round turban-cap and carries toys in the hand.

* The corporation accounts for 1763 note the gift of twelve "*pots de bièrre*" to those who carried the giant.

This singular group, which originating in one figure, has been added to from time to time, has survived, observes M. Quenson, "in spite of the advance of ages, the *mandements* of bishops, the edicts of councils, the murmurs of the pious, or the irony of the eighteenth century." To understand this, we must briefly allude to the eventful history of Gayant.

His real origin is shrouded in the mists of fable. He is popularly believed to have done good service in saving Douai in the time of Baldwin the Second, when besieged by Norman enemies; by creating a division at the head of his men and so preserving the city. Another traditionary tale goes, that he was a certain Jehan Gélon, Seigneur de Cantin, who resided in a castle near the town, having a subterranean communication between both places;

G

that he came through it to the conquered
inhabitants; placed himself at their head;
surprised their enemies, fatigued by car-
nage, and stupefied by wine; and, by a
general massacre, delivered the country.
The time of his advent in the public
shows has not been satisfactorily ascertained
by M. Quenson, nor do the archives of
the municipality, which he has consulted
with diligence, assist him. But the procession in which he usually figured was
instituted at the close of the fifteenth
century, in honor of the patron saint of
the city, St. Maurand. Douai, in the
early part of the next century, was dis-
tinguished as the Athens of Flanders,
and in the taste of that age, fostered by
Philippe-le-Bon, delighted in the glories
of public display; the accounts of expen-
diture preserved in the corporation records

show that no niggard hand dispensed
money in wines and feastings on these
occasions. It was not until 1665 that the
giantess appeared, and the accounts already
alluded to show that both were attended
by musicians and dancers, triumphal cars,
a figure of a dragon, and other pageants.
All of them were paraded in extra glory
in July, 1667, when Louis XIV and his
Queen made a "solemn entry" into Douai,
and the giants occasioned much amusement
to their Majesties by their quaint appearance. They are described in an account
of the festivities published at this time as
"deux grands colosses des deux sexes, d'une
prodigeuse hauteur et d'une industrie toute
particulière." At the close of the century,
the family of the giants, a son and daughter,
made their appearance. M. Quenson says,
"the giants of Flanders and Belgium

for the most part obtained progeny." It
was not, however, till 1715 that the third,
Binbin, appeared. In 1699, the Archbishop
of Arras suddenly issued a mandate forbidding their public display in religious
processions as heretofore. Great was the
grief of the people of Douai, when the
giants, St. Michael and the Devil, the
wheel of fortune, and .their other popular
shows were denounced as only fit to "irriter
la colère de Dieu :" the Archbishop ends
by forbidding, under pain of excommuni-
cation, any of the citizens to bear in their
processions, either in city or country,
figures of giants and the like " en habits
travestis," which he declares to be more
fit for the pagans, or the theatre ; and
" tout-à-fait opposés à l'esprit de l'Eglise."
A compromise was ultimately effected :
the religious part of the ceremony was

separated from the secular; and the
giants paraded Douai as usual. So great
was the love of the people for their fête
and their giant, that he was affectionately
termed *grand-père*, and a convivial society
of the principal inhabitants met under
the name of *Enfants de Gayant*. In 1770,
another Bishop of Arras interfered (urged
by the Proctor of the Ecclesiastical Court),
to stop the usual fêtes, which the people
were busy preparing. They all became
furious; the Town Council met, they
declared their giants, &c., were simply
intended for "honest recreation," and did
not deserve ecclesiastical intolerance. A
paper war commenced on both sides: the
magistrates argued for the antiquity of their
custom, but the Bishop prevailed, and
obtained the confirmation of the King
in June, 1771, to his mandate for the

suppression of the pageantry. In 1779,
the whole burst forth again in new splen-
dour; the gigantic family were repaired,
fully rehabited in the most fashionable
costume of that era, and a fourth child
added in a go-cart, which was personated
by the tallest man to be hired. The
Great Revolution again consigned them
for some years to obscurity and partial
decay; but in 1801 they were once more
brought forth, thoroughly repaired, and
newly dressed; the giantess being in the
first fashion of that era, with a short
waisted gown, a turban-hat and feather,
scarf, and reticule in hand. Around them
danced their three children, they themselves
moving in cadence to the voices of the
parties withinside who joined in chorus,
to the favourite air of Gayant, the very
popular song of the Douaisiens. Songs,

poems, and dramas, recorded the event;
and they peaceably paraded every year
until 1821, when they were again restored
and rehabited as exhibited in our cut.

Such is the history of the vicissitudes of
a great popular show. Having bestowed
thus much attention on the two principal
civic pageants of this kind on the continent,
we will more briefly allude to the gigantic
figures displayed elsewhere.

Malines, in a spirit of rivalry to Antwerp,
exhibited a figure in position and costume
very similar to the Antigonus of the latter
city. This giant was seated on a pedestal,
habited as an ancient Roman, and was
thirty feet in height. He (like the Douai
one) rejoiced in the popular name *Le Grand-
Papa ;* and on festival days was dragged
about the city on a car shaped like an
architectural platform, decorated with masks

and pendent wreaths, and drawn by four
powerful horses. In addition, a whole
family of giants marched on foot, consisting of a father and mother, two daughters
of different ages, and a young son. They
all wore a fantastic semi-Chinese costume.

Brussels had also its family of giants,
formerly consisting of a grand-papa, grand-
mama; their children, termed papa and

88a

GOLIATH AND HIS WIFE,
THE GIANTS OF ATH.

mama; and their grandchildren, two infants, popularly known as Jean, and Marie. The elders of the family have disappeared, and our cut represents all that remains of their descendants.

The giant of Ath rejoices in the formidable name of Goliath, and is of immense proportions; he is armed with a broadsword, and a mighty club furnished with spikes. His head is protected by a helmet, and his body by a breastplate; but from the waist downwards he takes the feminine appearance all these monsters possess, owing to the necessity of an abundance of drapery to conceal the men within who move the figure. Goliath's wife is an equally enormous figure, habited in the costume of the last century. This ancient name was not sacred to the giant of Ath; that of Nieuport bore the very same; the city of Troyes also formerly had its Goliath, who, on the entry of Charles VIII. to that city, in 1486, "very much diverted the King," as the old chronicler relates, in a scene with David, who ultimately brought him down by a stroke from his sling.

The giants of Louvain are also a wedded pair, but they indulge in the classic names of Hercules and his spouse Megara.

At Dunkirk, the giant is habited as a Spanish halberdier, of the time of Philip IV.; his wife is dressed in the style of the last century; their son, *Cupido*, is completely armed, like a knight for the tourney, mounted on a war-horse whose caparison hid the wheels and the men who pushed them along. The giant (forty-five feet in height) carried in his pocket one of the largest men to be hired, who

occasionally peeped out, shook his rattle,
and called to his *papa* or *maman*.

At Cassel, the giant is habited in the
costume of a warrior of the middle ages,
and followed by a very tall man dressed
as a baby.

At Ypres, and at Poperinghe, the giants
have also babies in their suite.

At Hazebrouck, the giant is in the
habit of a Turk, and is accompanied by
an elephant. His size is not equal to
the rest of his brethren, as one man
carries him; the body to the waist resting
on his shoulders; a long petticoat conceals
the legs.

The giant of Asselt is termed *Lange-
Man*. He was repaired for the Jubilee
of 1835; and was carried about the city
in a car, drawn by four horses; resting at
stated places, where soup was distributed,

in memory of a famine which afflicted
the city in the year 1638.

At Lille, the giants paraded the town
on all important occasions, and were last
repaired for the great communal fête of
that city in 1821.   Like others, they are
connected with old popular stories.   One
represents Lyderic, the first Grand Forester
of Flanders; the other his enemy, the cruel
Giant Phinart, whom he fought with and
conquered, beneath the walls of the
Chateau du Buc, which stood where the
good city of Lille was afterwards erected.
Our cut displays this redoubtable champion
as then exhibited; the numerous feet
seen, belong to his bearers withinside.
When the grand historic cortége passed
through the streets of the town in 1852,
these giants were followed by a group of
semi-barbarous warriors, dressed in skins of

LYDERIC,
GRAND FORESTER OF FLANDERS,
THE GIANT OF LILLE.

92b

beasts, and armed with stakes and maces.
Some were mounted on powerful horses,
drawing a car, upon which the story of
the early life of Lyderic was exhibited in
accordance with popular fable. A gigantic
female, named Jeanne Maillotte, appeared
in another part of the procession, decorated
with a military staff, and brandishing a
spear. She was accompanied by a grotesque tambour-major, and a corps of
drummers about seven feet in height.

Gigantic figures of animals also frequently
graced these shows; thus a colossal horse
named Bayard, upon which sat the four
sons of Aymon, the heroes of the once
famed mediæval romance, is carried about
the streets of Malines on the great anni-
versaries of St. Romuald, the patron saint
of the city, and is intended as " an emblem
of the union and fidelity of its inhabitants,"

typified in the model of fraternity displayed
by those fabulous heroes.

The *Fête du Poulain*, at Pezenas, in
Provence, was instituted in 1226, by Louis
VIII. The chief feature, the *Poulain*, is
a gigantic horse made of cardboard, covered
with real skin, with a mane and tail tied
up with variegated ribands, and housings
of blue enriched with gold *fleurs-de-lis*. It
is moved by two men withinside, and surrounded by a gay group of richly-clad
dancers, who promenade the town, exe-
cuting their dances at stated intervals.

Enormous camels and unicorns, sea-mon-
sters of fabulous origin and fanciful design,
likethe "licorne" and sea-horse—all having
some local significance—were, and are, still
paraded. But of all monsters the dragon
has been the most universally popular,
rivalling, or even surpassing the giants

themselves. Dragons had a general religious significance, but were frequently connected with the legendary career of some
local saint. In their general meaning, they
conveyed an idea of the evil spirit, of
sorcery, or heresy. Thus in many of the
churches of France before the great Revolution, it was customary, three days before
Holy Thursday, for the clergy to carry in
procession a dragon, whose long tail was
filled with chaff. The first two days it was
borne *before* the cross, with the tail *full;*
the third day it was borne *after* the cross
with the tail *empty:* this was intended to
signify that on the first days the devil
reigned in the world; but that on the last
he was dispossessed. The local dragons
abounded, and were realizations of those
believed to have been conquered by the
patron saints of various places. M. Bottin,

in his *History of the North of France,* has
noted twenty-one such in that district alone;
and M. Delmotte, in his *Recherches sur
Gilles de Chin et le Dragon de Mons,* has
added seventeen others; which are very far
from completing a perfect list. The dragons
of St. Margaret and St. George form part
of their legendary history; those of Mons
and Rouen are believed to be typical of
localities sacred to the church.*   With
ourselves, dragons of monstrous size were
as popular as giants; and I may here introduce as a curiosity the last of the English

* Thus Gilles de Chin, who fought with the dragon
of Mons, founded the Abbey of Wasmes, on a tract of
marsh land (*wame* in the Walloon dialect), which pes-
tiferous spot was symbolized by the dragon. Louis de
Sacy in the same way explained the dragon of Rouen,
conquered by St. Romain, as a type of the irruption of
water prevented by him. This dragon was termed, *la
gargouille,* a term still applied to the water-spouts of
churches, often made in the form of a dragon.

dragons which belonged to the corporation
of Norwich, and was always carried in
Mayoralty processions, until the Reform
Bill, in 1832, finally conquered the monster.
St. George and St. Margaret were the
patron saints of the old Guilds of this city,
therefore the dragon had a double hold on
popular sympathy; and was popularly known
as *snap* or *snap-dragon*.

The body of this monster was formed of
light materials, being composed of canvas
stretched over a framework of wood; the

H

outside was painted of a sea-green colour, with gilt scales, picked out with red. The body was five feet in length, and was sometimes used to secrete wine abstracted from the Mayor's cellars. The neck was capable of elongation (measuring three feet and a half when extended), was supported by springs attached to the body, and was capable of being turned in any direction at the will of the bearer. From between the ears the whole outer extremity of the back was surmounted by a sort of mane, of crimson colour, tied in fantastic knots around the juncture of the enormous tail, which extended above five feet, curling at the further extremity, as exhibited in the cut (a). Between the wings was a small aperture for air, and beneath the body was hung a sort of petticoat, to conceal the legs of the bearer, whose feet were furnished with large claws.

The dragon's head had its lower jaw
furnished with a plate of iron resembling a
horse-shoe; it was formerly garnished with
enormous nails, which produced a terrible

clatter when the jaws met together.   They
were made to open and shut by means of
strings, and the children amused themselves
by throwing halfpence into the gaping mouth,
which turned to the right and left during
the whole of the journey, noisily clashing its

jaws, from which the Dragon's popular name
of *snap* was probably derived.

Giants, like dragons, were regarded as
emblematic of an evil principle; they type-
fied paganism in its most repulsive form, if
indeed they may not be, as some writers
imagine, derived from the rites of paganism
itself. Dr. Milner, in his *History of Winchester*, 1798, takes this view of the question,
when speaking of the huge wicker figures in
which the Gauls enclosed and burnt their
victims as a sacrifice to their gods. He says:
" In different places on the opposite side of
the channel, where we are assured that the
rites in question prevailed, among the rest at
Dunkirk and Douay, it has been an immemorial custom on a certain holiday in the
year, to build up an immense figure of
basketwork and canvas to the height of forty
or fifty feet, which, when properly painted

and dressed, represented a huge giant, which also contained a number of living men within it, who raised the same, and caused it to move from place to place. The popular tradition was, that this figure represented a certain pagan giant, who used to devour the inhabitants of these places, until he was killed by a patron saint of the same. Have not we here a plain trace of the horrid sacrifices of Druidism offered up to Saturn, or Moloch, and of the beneficial effect of Christianity in destroying the same? " In the great procession on the festival of Corpus Christi giants were commonly seen. In the *Life of Friar Gerund*, the author alludes to the boys going " after the giants and the serpent Tarasca,* on the day of Corpus;"

* " *La Tarasque* " was the name given to the dragon yearly paraded about the old City of Tarascon, in the south of France.—*Dulaure's Hist. de Paris.*

and, in an explanatory note, we are told "the figures of gigantic men and a large serpent are carried about on this day, by way of showing the conquest of Christ over the powers of earth and hell. The serpent is called *Taraka*, say the etymologists, from τεραξ *unde* τὸ τεραστιον, and *in plur.* τὰ τεραστια, *monstra, portenta, miracula.** In the relation of the Earl of Nottingham's journey into Spain (*Harleian Miscellany*, vol. 3, p. 420) is a description of the great Corpus Christi procession at Valladolid, in 1604, in which the King walked, bearing a lighted taper; and in which procession "first came eight great giants, three men and three women, and two Moors, with a tabor and pipe playing, and they dancing." The Church of Rome possessed one saintly giant,

* See p. 61 for a notice, by Dr. Plot, of the custom of carrying a giant and dragon in Oxfordshire.

who was frequently exhibited on this occa·
sion. Naogeorgus, in his *Popish Kingdom*,
as translated by Barnaby Googe, tells us,
that amid the general display on the festival
of Corpus Christi,—

> "Great Christopher doth wade and passe with Christ
> amid the brook."

The old history of St. Christopher, as related in Caxton's translation of Voragine's
Golden Legend, 1483, assures us, that he
was "of a right grete stature, and had a
terryble and ferdful chere and countenaunce ;
and he was twelve cubytes of length." He
was converted by a hermit to Christianity, and
by him induced to devote himself to carrying
travellers safely over a dangerous stream.
One night, while sleeping, he was awakened
by the voice of a child, who desired to be
carried across. The giant lifted the child

on his shoulders, and entered the river;
but the waters rose higher and higher, and
the child waxed heavier each foot he strode.
With much trouble he landed him, saying:
" Child, thou hast put me in great peril;
thou weighest almost as if I had borne the
whole world: I could bear no greater bur-
den." And the child answered: " Christopher, marvel not! thou hast borne more
than that, for thou hast borne him that
made it on thy shoulders. I am the Christ
whom thou servest in thy work." Figures
of this saint were constantly painted on
church walls, and sometimes at the entrance of cities, for it was a popular belief,
as noted by Erasmus in his *Praise of
Folly*, that the day on which his figure was
seen, a violent death, or a death without confession, could not happen to the
spectator.

The engraving here given is copied from the
only representation known to the author, of
this popular saint, as exhibited on this equally
popular festival. It occurs among the plates
to the *Explication des Cérémonies de la Fête-*

Dieu d'Aix en Provence, 1777. This celebrated fête, founded by the old troubadour King
of Jerusalem and Count of Provence—the far-
famed Réné of Anjou—in the early part of

the fifteenth century, retained, until the
time of the publication of the volume just
alluded to, many of its ancient features.
This of St. Christopher being one of the
most curious, and described as "having the
body formed of hoops of wood, enveloped
in a long white dress, the arms extended
in the form of a cross, a figure of the infant
Saviour seated on the right one. The figure
was nine or ten feet in height, and carried
by a man withinside, who kept what
sailors call "a bright look out" for the
liberal pious, when he made the figure
courteously salute them, and so " obtained
a little more   silver   in   return for this
politeness."

Such is a brief record of the giants, reli-

---

* The giant of the Tailors' Company at Salisbury, was
one popularly known as St. Christopher, though without
the proper attributes of that converted giant. See p. 62.

gious and secular, at home and abroad. It may serve to show the popularity of the fabulous history of old cities.

The people of the Low Countries still cling to theirs, and proudly exhibit their legendary giants. We have long since forgotten our fables; they lie in the seldom read pages of Geoffry of Monmouth. We now no longer, when the Sovereign of England dines with the Lord Mayor, remind him in boastful rhymes that London is Troynovant, or New Troy, founded by Brutus long before Christ, and claiming precedence of Rome. But all this was complacently done as late as the middle of the seventeenth century. My object in this volume has been to rescue my old friends Gog and Magog from the contemptuous slights of such as know not their origin; and do not feel how curiously they are

linked with mediæval observances at home
and abroad, with the history of our native
City, and the glories of its great popular ruler,
my Lord Mayor, in the days long past,—

"When London did pour out her citizens,
The Mayor and all his brethren in best sort."

Addenda.

ADDENDA.

Page 9.—THE INVASION OF BRUTUS.

This legendary history of early Britain, as well
as the detailed account of the battle with the
giants, and the same repeated in the *History of
Fulke Fitz-Warine* (pp.18—20), may be all traced
to the *British History* of Geoffry of Monmouth;
an absurd collection of fanciful tales brought
together by him in the early part of the twelfth
century, from the Welsh traditions, and dedi-
cated to the use of Robert of Gloucester, natural
son of King Henry I.

The amazing clearness of detail this historian

gives to events which happened in pre-historic times, delighted for many ages a certain class of romantic readers. In it we have such documents as " correct copies " of letters written by the imaginary Brutus of Troy, at the time when Eli governed Israel; while the speeches of himself and his officers are given with the accuracy of a modern parliamentary reporter. His labours in thus constructing a history, where no true history existed, met, however, a grateful reward. His work was widely read, particularly by our early poets ; the noblest of them all here found the substructure of his *King Lear*.

The graver historians of the Shakespearian era by no means cast aside the tales of reverend Geoffry ; they were taken as facts by eminent men ; even the learned Camden confesses to a wavering over them, and, in the early part of his *Britannia*, excuses himself from condemning what had been so long received as truths. When ultimately discarded by the learned, the

tales were treasured by the populace, and repro-
duced in cheap books as " reverend histories."

For the more immediate convenience of the
reader, we here give Geoffry's description of the
encounter between Corineus and Gogmagog.
He prefaces the account by telling us that when
Brutus first invaded Albion it was inhabited by
none but a few giants. Corineus had for his
share of the land the county of Cornwall; the
rest we tell in Geoffry's words:

" It was a great diversion to Corineus to
encounter the said giants, which were in greater
numbers there than in all the other provinces
that fell to the share of his companions. Among
the rest was one detestable monster, named
Goëmagot, in stature twelve cubits, and of such
prodigious strength, that at one shake he pulled
up an oak as if it had been a hazel wand. On
a certain day, when Brutus was holding a solemn
festival to the gods, in the port where they at
first landed, this giant with twenty more of

I

his companions came in upon the Britons, among whom he made a dreadful slaughter. But the Britons at last assembling together in a body, put them to the rout, and killed them every one but Goëmagot. Brutus had given orders to have him preserved, out of a desire to see a combat between him and Corineus, who took a great pleasure in such encounters. Corineus, overjoyed at this, prepared himself, and throwing aside his arms, challenged him to wrestle with him. At the beginning of the encounter, Corineus and the giant, standing front to front, held each other strongly in their arms, and panted aloud for breath; but Goëmagot presently grasping Corineus with all his might, broke three of his ribs, two on his right side, and one on his left. At which Corineus, highly enraged, roused up his whole strength, and snatching him upon his shoulders, ran with him as fast as the weight would allow him, to the next shore, and there getting upon the top of a high rock, hurled down the savage monster into the sea; where, falling on the sides of craggy rocks, he was torn to pieces, and coloured the waves with his blood. The place where he fell, taking its name from the giant's fall, is called Lam Goëmagot, that is, Goëmagot's Leap, to this day."

Dr. Giles, in his edition of this old Chronicle, tells us, that this spot "is now called the Haw, and is near Plymouth."

Page 11.—GOG AND MAGOG.

The names of Gog and Magog are first found in the Old Testament. Magog is named as one of the sons of Japheth in the tenth chapter of Genesis; and again in the first book of Chronicles, chap. 1, v. 5. Magog is not associated with Gog until the times of Ezekiel, during the

Captivity, from the thirtieth year of Nabopalassar, 595, B.C., down to 572, B.C. (Ezekiel xxxviii, 2; xxxix. 6.) In the post-Christian but uncertain age of the writer of the Apocalypse (between A.D. 95 and the Council of Laodicea, which rejected it as apocryphal, 360—369, A.D.), "Gog and Magog appear together as *nations* (Revelations xx. 20); whereas, seven or eight centuries previously, Gog, the Prince of Rhos, Meshech, and Tubal would seem to have been understood as the proper name of a King."— Nott and Gliddon, *Types of Mankind*, Philadelphia, 1857, p. 470.

Page 15.—GIGANTIC HEROES.

In addition to the gigantic heroes mentioned here and on page 2, it may be worth noting the names of Charlemagne and Godfrey de Bouillon, for whose great deeds mediæval fancy awarded great stature. The fabulous Roland was also a giant. For further remarks on the subject, see Leroux de Lincy, *Liv. des Legendes*, t. 1. p. 153—5.

Page 16.—BOREMAN AND HIS BOOKS.

It appears that Thomas Boreman, whose stall was near the two Giants in Guildhall, throve well by publishing his first tiny volume of their "*Gigantick History*," for in the preface to the second, which completes the history of the Guildhall, the chapel adjoining, "and other curious matters," relative to Mayoralty cere-monials, he says: "*Necessity*, the mother of *Invention*, was the author of the first part; which, as soon as she had finish'd, left me, and sent *success* in her stead; now, this last lady and I had been long strangers, and, altho' she has lived with me about three months, we know not how to behave to each other: in short, she is a very desirable person, but much fitter for pleasure than business. *Necessity*, for invention and dispatch, is worth two of her; and if the latter had not stept back again to begin the work, I fear the former, whose task it was, would never have finished it." He apologizes for his *two* volumes, because one may be put in the pocket of each subscriber, and "there would be no fear of their growing lapsided from the weight of such a gigantic work." Among his list of subscribers he inserts the name of " Giant Corineus" for " 100 books," and " Giant Gogmagog" for the same number.

He continued a series of volumes of the same size and price, making nine in all. Two devoted to the history of St. Paul's Cathedral, and two more to the Tower of London. In 1742, he

published one entitled *The History of Cajanus,
the Swedish Giant, from his birth to the present
time. By the author of the Gigantick Histories.*
He afterwards published two volumes on West-
minster Abbey, but required an advance on the
price of each volume, which was raised to sixpence.

Page 21.—JAJIOUGE AND MAJIOUGE.

Nott and Gliddon, in their *Types of Mankind*
(Philadelphia, 1857, p. 470), say: " Arab tradition, under the appellatives *Yadjooj* and *Mad-
jooj,* prolongs the union [of the elder Scriptural
Gog and Magog] down to the seventh century
after Christ; with the commentary that they
are two nations descended from Japheth; *Gog*
being attributed to the Turks, and *Magog* to the

Geelàn, the Geli and Gelæ of Ptolemy and Strabo, and our *Alarni*.

"In ancient Greek and Latin, *Gigas*, read also *Gug*-as, signified *giant*; and oriental legend associated giants with Scythians in the north of Asia. *Magog* has been assimilated to the *Massagetæ* [perhaps *Massa-Getæ*, *Masian-Getæ*, of Mount *Masuis*] who are to Getæ what *Magog* is to *Gog*; the prefixes *ma* and *massa* being considered intensitives, to indicate either the most honoured branch of the nation, or the whole nation itself."

The authors adopt the opinion of Dubois, who says "the Hebrew word is *Ma-gug*. The first syllable refers to the *Maiotes*, Tauric Medians, transplanted from the Taurus to the east of the Caspian. The second syllable, *Gug*, is simply the Indo-Germanic word *Khogh*, or mountain. "Having thus fixed *Gug* to a mountain, *Cauc*-asos, the root of *Asos* is instantly recognised in the natural name of the *Osses*,

Osseth, Yases, Aas, Asi; whence the continent of Asia derives its Europeon designation. As far back as history mounts, she finds within the angle circumscribed between the Caucasus, the Palus Méotis, and the Tanais, an Asia proper, inhabited by a people, 'As,' of Indo-Germanic race: and we discover in the *Ma*-iotes of the 'mountain' *Cauc*-asus, the long-lost, and mystified nation, *Ma-Gug* of the tenth chapter of Genesis."

Page 60.—THE COVENTRY GIANTS.

The following detailed accounts of the expenses incurred by the two Coventry companies who indulged in giants, is given from Sharp's volume. The first is especially valuable, as it shows the constant repair, &c., required by the figure, year by year, for twenty years.

1533.	Item.	Payed for the Gyant . . xxvij^{s.}	viij^{d.}

1533. Item. Payed for the Gyant . . xxvijᵃ· viijᵈ·
1534. —— —— — dressyng the Gyant —— vi.
—— —— — beryng the Gyant —— xii.
—— —— — naylls and corde —— ij.
—— —— — painte . . —— j.
1540. —— —— — pentteng of the } Gyant . . . . } v. —
—— —— — the candelsteke } in hys hed and the lyght } —— ij.
—— —— — bereng of the Gyant —— xvij.
1542. P'd for kepyng the Gyant (inter alia)
1547. Beryng of the Gyant ij. nyghts . ij —
P'd for waxe candell for the Gyant . — j.
Item. Paid for canvas to make the } Gyant a newe skerte . } — ix.
—— —— — pentyng of the } Gyant . . . . } iij. viij.
1548. Paid for the Gyeande (bearing) . — xvi.
—— — mendyng of the Gyeande . — viij.
1549. —— — beryng the Joyand . . — xviij.
For mendyng of hys head and arme — xvj.
1551. Dressyng and mendyng of the } Gyeande . . . . . } — xviij.
Payd for a candell for the Gyeande . — ij.
1553. For mendyng the Gyeand . . — xxij.
Mendying and payntyng the Gyand ij. vj.

DRAPER'S ACCOUNT.

1556.	Payd to Robart Crowe for makyng of the Gyanes	xx⁴.	—
1556.	Payed to ij men for beryng of the Gyenes	—	xxijᵈ.
1557.	—— — payntyng of the Gyenes wyffe	ij.	iiij.
	—— — the beryng of the Gyans wyffe	—	xviij.
1560.	—— — pentyng of the Gyans wyffe	ij.	vj.
	—— to endes for the waxe	v.	—

Page 79.—GAYANT, THE GIANT OF DOUAI.

The name *Gayant* (which by M. M. Baudry
and Durot has been thought to signify *the
Dragon*), now assumed as the proper name
of the great figure of Douai, is the pure
mediæval form of the word *giant*; as proved
by M. Delmotte, in the following quotations

from old romances : many more might be
cited if necessary.

> " Ains mais si biaus hom ne fu nés ;
> Il n'est pas meures d'un *galant*."
> *Roman de Perceval.*

> " Caïens est un *galans*, biau sire."
> *Ibid.*

> " Mieux vaut un *jayant* que un page,
> Et deux dismes que un terrage."
> *Jeu-Parti.* (Chanson 28.)

Page 83.—EXPENSES OF THE DOUAI GIANT.

The following extracts from the archives of
Douay, are selected from the work of M.
Quenson, and detail the expenses incurred

by the municipality on the occasion of the
display of the giants, June 10, 1665.

	Flor-ins.	Pas-tars.
A cinq homes ayans porte le geant, paye a chascun 30 past. faisant	7	10
A ceulx ayans portez la geante pour ceste fois seullement pour estre a la charge des mandeliers	„	30
Aux deux garçons ayans dansez devant le geant et la geante	„	20
A Martin Mauduy pour douze paires de souliers blancs livrez pour joustes et danses par devant le geant et la geante paye par reduction	6	16
Au Sr. Laurent Durieu eschevin pour diverses parties de grosseries tant pour l'habit de la geante, estendart qualtrement selon son billet	283	13
A Philippe Blassel pour la facon de l'habit de la geante et aultres petitz habitz apparant par son billet reduict a	32	„
A Marie Jenne Paul pour avoir faict la perruque de la geante, raccomode celle du geant et St. Michel, paye par reduction . . .	17	„

	Flor-ins.	Pas-res.

A Guillaume Gourbé mandelier pour la facon
　　et livreson d'osier tant pour la geante que
　　pour le bracquet et marteau d'armes, et
　　r'accommode le geant　.　.　.　. 31 — „

A M. Loys Cardon pour avoir faict les pieds et
　　mains de St. Michel et le carguant de la
　　geante, payé　.　.　.　.　.　. 3 — „

Pour vingt et une cordes de perles applicquez
　　a la coiffure de la geante, a 3 past. chascuns
　　paye enssemble　.　.　.　.　. „ — 63

Pour avoir moulle la teste de la geante construit
　　ses mains, son collier, sa rose de diamant
　　et diverses aultres pieches d'ornement, passe 40 — „

————

Page 86.—RESTORATION OF GAYANT.

The serio-comic poem on the restoration of
the giant of Douai, in 1779, to his affectionate
friends, the inhabitants of that city, is here
given from the appendix to the work of

M. Quenson, so frequently quoted. It was composed by M. Seraphin Bernard, " Greffier de la Mairie de Douai," and printed in 4to, 1780, by M. Derbaix, who was executed " à la lanterne," in the Revolution of 1793. It may be worth noting here, that during the same horrible period, it was the custom with the *concierge* of the Hotel de Ville, during the three *fête* days, to exhibit the heads of Gayant and his family on the balcony of that building.

LA PROCESSION DE DOUAI,

Ou Gayant Resuscité.

Jadis j'aurais chanté le tombeau de Gayant ;
Je célèbre aujourd'hui son triomphe éclatant.

Muse, qui du béfroi vis la reconnaissance,
Le zèle, les regrets, la solide éloquence,
Rapeller notre perte et ranimer nos cœurs,
Viens orner mes écrits, y répandre des fleurs.
Ecarte loin de moi cette image cruelle,
Ces rapports destructeurs, qu'inspira le faux zèle,

Que du haut d'un clocher tu vis tracer exprès,
Pour répandre le deuil au milieu de la paix ;
Eloigne aussi de moi tout accent de tristesse :
Gayant ressuscité ramène l'allégresse.

Ce héros mémorable, objet de tous tes vœux,
Agréable signal des plaisirs et des jeux ;
Que le sort a détruit, que le sort fait renaître,
Douai, réjouis-toi, ton Gayant va paroitre !
Je le vois s'élever, sortir de son tombeau.
Triomphant de la mort, fût-il jamais si beau ?
Sur son front glorieux, un casque redoubtable,
Rapelle la valeur de son bras formidable ;
Ses nobles vêtemens, ornemens des guerriers,
Annoncent ses exploits, ses antiques lauriers.*
Gayant va se venger !—Non.   La paix, qui l'inspire,
Veut qu'au bonheur commun aujourd'hui tout conspire ;
La vengeance n'est point dans ses doux sentimens ;
Ses ennemis vaincus vont être ses enfans.
Semblable à ces Gaulois, dont le mâle courage,
Par la force accablé, savait braver l'orage ;
De leurs fiers ennemis ils repoussaient les traits,
Et, vainqueurs généreux, ils leur donnaient la paix.
Ansi Gayant, tombé sous les coups de l'envie,
Redeviant généroux en reprenant la vie :

* Suivant la tradition populaire, Gayant a défendée Douai.

Il sait que la clémence illustre les héros,
Et qu'il faut pardonner à d'orgueilleux rivaux.

Venez, Douaisiens ! venez, Peuple fidéle !
Contemplez *sa grandeur* et sa gloire immortelle ;
Livrez-vous à la joye, appellez les plaisirs :
Le plus heureux succès couronne vos désirs.

Et vous, Peuples voisins ! qui, depuis sa disgrâce,
Six ans nous avez fuis, venez, sa dédicace,
Ramène avec les jeux, les festins, l'amitié.
Si sa perte en vos cœurs avis mis la pitié,
Qu'elle en sorte à jamais.   Que sa joyeuse fête,
Vous fasse partager la gaieté qu'elle apprête.

Déjà l'airain sonnant annonce la splendeur
Du jour trois fois heureux, qu'aspire avec ardeur.
Le Peuple qui l'aima, le grand qui le souhaite ;
Enfin tout est content, et la joie est parfaite.
La villageois s'éveille, et quittant son hameau,
Assemble ses amis, monte sur le côteau,
Contemple la Cité, vers ses murs s'achemine ;
Il a pris en passant *Agathe* sa voisine.
Sur la route ils ont joint *Guillaume, Alain, Pierrot,*
Et le viellard *Antoine,* et l'antique *Margot.*
Ceux-ci font de Gayant une histoire fidèle :
Ils disent qu'à sa fête une ardeur mutuelle,

K

Les enflama tous deux, et que leur union
Commença leur bonheur à sa procession.
Les amans, à ces mots, disent à leurs maitresses,
Que depuis bien long-tems leur constantes tendresses
Vainement ont parlé.   Qu'aujourd'hui leur bonheur,
Doit leur être assuré par un aveu du cœur ;
Que cette occasion veut qu'ils se réjouissant,
Et qu'ils doivent s'aimer.—Les viellards applaudissent.
Tandis que ces discours repandant la gaieté,
Tous ces bons villageois ont gagné la cité.

   Les bourgeois étrangers répandent la gaité,
Renfermés, ils ont dû voir le grand jour éclore.
Les ponts sont abaisses.   Je les vois pétillans,
Accourir à grand flots sur des chars éclatans,
Confier leurs destins à l'élément liquide,*
En braver la fureur, l'inconstance perfide ;
D'autres par des sentiers précipiter leurs pas.
Tous brûleut d'arriver : Gayant leur tend les bras.
L'un d'avance le loue et l'autre le déprise ;
L'un dit sa femme est bien, sa fille est moin bien mise ;
Binbin est bien coiffé, son habit est usé ;
L'aine dans ses habits a l'air embarrassé.
Voilà comme toujours, enclins à la satyre,
Les hommes, sans juger, commencent par médire.

* La Barque.

Mais quel nouveau spectacle attire mes regards ?

De jeunes combattans* viennent de toutes parts.

Des diverses cités, des hameaux, c'est l'élite :

Chacun de son côté range la réussite.

Ils sont prêts au combat ; le cirque va s'ouvrir†

Jeunesse, combattez, suivez votre désir.

Le signal est donné. Dans les airs élancée,

La balle par dix mains aussitot repoussée,

Par d'autres est rendue : arrêtée à la fin,

Elle a fait des jouers le sort et le destin.

La Scarpe des long-tems au deuil abandonnée,

Entend les cris de joie, en demeure étonnée ;

Elle voit sur les bords l'espoir, le Dieu des jeux,

Animer un spectacle agréable à ses yeux.

A cette heureuse vue, appellant l'allégresse,

Elle passe aux transports de la plus douce ivresse.

Aux acclamations d'un peuple transporté,

Aux sons des instrumens qui marquent la gaîté,

Pénétrant à travers la foule réjouie,

Conduit par la Fortune, image de la vie ;

Gayant, accompagné de sa femme, de ses fils,

S'avance vers la place et s'arrête au Parvis.

Là contemplant d'un œil satisfait et tranquille,

Les peuples de Douai, Valencienne, et Lille,

* Jouers de Balle. † L'Esplanade.

K 2

D'Arras, Tournai, Cambrai, de Béthune, et Bouchain,
Des hameaux d'alentour, rassemblés tous enfin ;
Il se sent pénétré de la reconnaissance,
Il parle, et dans l'instant règne au profond silence !

" O joie! ô doux transports, mes enfans, mes amis !
Je renais au bonheur, vous voyant réunis.
Jadis,—le souvenir m'en fait frémir encore,
Jadis le sort cruel, pour des faits que j'ignore,
En me privant du jour, attrista mes enfans,
Et nous ravit à tous nos plaisirs les plus grands.
Maintenant que je vis, maintenant que l'orage,
Pleinement dissipé, laisse un jour sans nuage,
Sentons le prix du calme après tant des malheurs,
Livrons-nous au plaisir, savourons ses douceurs,
Oublions pour jamais les noirs traits de l'envie,
Ne songeons qu'à jouir des instans de la vie.
Je vais porter la joie á tous les habitants,
Les voir, les visiter et les rendre contents.
Mes adieux autrefois, dictés par la détresse,
Portèrant dans les cœurs la deuil et la tristesse.
Il faut que ma présence y porte la gaité,
Et que d'un plaisir par chacun soit transporté."
Ainsi parla Gayant. Il part. Les cris de joie
Se font entendre au loin. Le plaisir se déploie.
Le cri : " Vive, Gayant," est cent fois répété ;
Et l'on se divertit dans toute la cité.

O vous, restaurateurs da plaisir populaire,
Magistrats ! recevez mon hommage sincère.
Né dans votre cité, j'essayi près des vous
De célèbre les jeux revenus parmi nous,
Et des Douaisiens de chanter des merveilles.
En publiant ces vers, faible fruit de mes vielles,
" Si de vous agréer je n'emporte le prix,
Il est flatteur au moins de l'avoir enterpris."

Page 86.—THE SONG OF GAYANT.

The enthusiasm with which the people of Douai welcomed the second restoration of their giant in 1801, occasioned the production of many gratulatory poems and couplets; and among the rest, the song descriptive of the yearly festivities given below. It was printed in the *Etrennes Douaisiennes;* and is supposed to be the narration by a countryman of the neighbourhood, in his provincial *patois,* of the great doings which are so attractive to the whole district. The "wheel of fortune," alluded to in the fourth verse, is a very popular part of the pageantry, and has been introduced in other shows of the kind elsewhere, particularly in the Fête-Dieu at Aix, and the festival of St. Rombaud, at Malines. It consists of a plain wheel laid flat upon a car drawn by horses; in the centre is a figure of Fortune; and upon the outer circle, at the junction of each spoke, is placed a figure indicative of some grade in life, the soldier, priest, husbandman, &c. As the car is drawn, a rolling side-long movement is given to the wheel, which lifts or depresses the various figures as the wheel revolves. It is a simple moralization of human life, which easily appeals to the vulgar comprehension, and is consequently much relished by the country folks, who never tire in enforcing its meaning on the minds of their children. The air to

which the words of this song are sung rivals in
popularity that of Mons, described in a future
page; it is played by the *carillons*, by the
street musicians, and sung universally on this
joyous day.

CHANSON DE GAYANT.

Allons, veux-tu venir, compère,
A la ducasse de Douai :
Ah ! c'est si joli et si gai,
Que de Valenciennes et Tournai,
De Lille, d'Orchies, et d'Arras,
Les pas pressés viennent à grand pas.

Allons, di in pau men compère,
Ché qu'un y verra tout de bon,
Des jueux arrivant de long,
Avec fusicqs, arcs et boujons,
Et des jueux de balle aussi,
Ah ! men compère, t'en s'ras surpris.

Sur des plaches toutes nouvielles,
Y s'in vont disputer les prix :
A Saint-Amé avec fusicqs,
Saint-Nicolas avec arcs rodis,

Saint-Jacques c'est encor pus mieux,
T'y verras chelle balle et les jueux.

Je verras chelle bielle rue de fortune
Rouler et courir à grand pas :
C'est pour te dire que tout va,]
Et tantôt haut et tantôt bas,
Argentier, avocat, paysan,
Chacun ju rôle en courant.

Gayant arrive sur la grand' plache,
Avec sa femme et ses enfans,
Il dit a tous les habitans :
Divertissez-vous sagement.
Dans ces jours si biaux et si gais,
Vous pouvez tous boire à longs traits.

Wette in pau, compère v'là Jacques,
Avec Fillon qui danse si bin,
Et v'là là-bas ch'tiot Binbin
Qui ju au volant tout douchemin.
Turlututu v'là l'grand Gayant,
Tout en faisant des contre-tems.

V'là déjà tros heures qui sonnent,
Le ju de balle va commencher.
Allons-y d'un pas redoublé
Pour vir tons chés faraux juer.

L'un wette en haut, l'autre wette en bas,
Y sont plus subtils que de cats.

Au son des timballes et trompettes,
L'balle gagnée les prix donnés,
Chés amoureux iront, danser
A l'comédie, à l'Elisée,
Tous joyeux et tertous contens,
Turlututu, vive Gayant.

Page 88.—THE BRUSSELS GIANTS.

The legendary history of the giants of
Brussels, like that of other municipal figures of
their kind, is connected with the early foundation of the city. The legend relates that the
aboriginal giant and his wife, respectively
named Jan and Jannika, had resided in the
district in which Brussels now stands since the
period of the deluge. The advent of new
settlers, and the foundation of a walled city,
alarmed the worthy couple, who are traditionally

reported to have looked over the wall, forty feet
high, of what is now the Rue Villa Hermosa,
with no friendly eye upon the colony of human
dwarfs, who where ultimately destined to put
an end to the long reign of the giants in the
land.   This universal belief in a race of colossal
proportion, defeated by the ancestry of various
peoples, displays a love of the marvellous, combined with a fair share of vanity, in the ancient
prowess which gave victory to the modern races.

———

Page 96.—THE DRAGON OF MONS.

The festival at Mons was really founded in
memory of the relief of the inhabitants from a
great pest (*peste noire*), which ravaged the
country in 1348.   Now, as it was common in all
processions of the epoch to represent the evil
principle under the form of a dragon of osier, he

appeared with St. George, whose victim he
became after a fight in the great square. St.
George had upon the *arçon* of his saddle a
small figure of faith,—the *poupée* of the popular
song; for which the representation of the Virgin
and child has since been substituted,—*l'mama*
of the same verses. The *Doudou* is the name
given to the dragon; and the following are the
words of *L'ancien Noel du Doudou*, as these
popular rhymes are termed by M. Delmotte:

LE DOU-DOU.

Nos irons vir l'car d'or
A l'procession de Mon;
Ce s'ra l'poupée Saint George,
Qui no' suivra de long;
C'est l'doudou, c'est l'mama
C'est l'poupée, poupée, poupée;
C'est l'doudou, c'est l'mama,
C'est l'poupée Saint George qui va,
Le gins du rempart riront com' des kiards,
De vir tant de carottes,
Le gins du culot riront com' de sots,
De vir tant de carot' à leu' pots.

The enthusiasm at Mons on these feast-days
is universal, and is best described in the lively
words of the French author: "Que lorsque les
premières notes du Doudou se font entendre sur
le carillon pendant la fête, la figure des habitants de Mons rayonne de joie; tout le monde
chante ou danse cet air chéri; des exclamations
presque frénétiques s'échappant au milieu des
éclats de rire, des gambades; quand on se
rencontre on se donne la main, ou invite même
les étrangers à manger de la tarte, du jambon,
etc.; c'est un délire universal. Cet air est aussi
célèbre à Mons que le fameux air de *Gayant* à
Douai."

Page 101.—GIANTS VANQUISHED BY SAINTS.

M. Delmotte, in his tract published anony-
mously at Mons, in 1825, and entitled *Recherches Historiques sur Gilles, Seigneur de Chin et*

le Dragon, has given the following list of the principal saints who have conquered dragons, according to their legendary history :

> Ste. Attracta.
>
> St. Benoit of Arezzo.
>
> St. Bienheuré of Vendôme.
>
> St. Derien of Landernau.
>
> St. Donatus.
>
> St. George.
>
> St. Gratus.
>
> St. Hilarion.
>
> St. Jacobus.
>
> St. Jean de Reaume.
>
> St. Jouin, Bishop of Le'on.
>
> St. Léon of Mans.
>
> Ste. Marguerite.
>
> Ste. Marthe of Tarascon.
>
> St. Marcel of Paris.
>
> St. Meen, Abbé of St. Florent.
>
> St. Michael the Archangel.
>
> St. Pavace of Mans.
>
> St. Peregrinus.
>
> St. Pol, Bishop of Léon.
>
> Ste. Radegonde of Poitiers.

St. Romain, Bishop of Rouen.

St. Samson, Bishop of Dole.

St. Theodorus.

Ste. Vénérande.

St. Victor of Marseilles.

St. Vigor.

To this he has added a still more curious list of the various French cities in which dragons are publicly paraded on the festival days of certain saints, appending references to books where full notices of such events occur :

"A Reims, *la kraulla*. (*Expilly*, article *Reims*.)

A Paris, le dragon de St. Marcel. (*Sauval*, livre ii.)

A Vendôme, le dragon de St. Bienheuré. (*Dulaure, Histoire de Paris.*)

A l'Abbaye de Fleury. (*Ducange*.)

A la Roche-Turpin, près Montoire. (*Dulaure, Hist. de Paris.*)

A Rouen. *la Gargouille*. (*Expilly*, article *Rouen*.)

A Poitiers, *la grande-gueule, ou la bonne Sainte-Vermine*. (*Dulaure, Hist. de Paris.*)

A Tarascon, *la Tarasque*. (Idem.)

A Troyes, *la chair salée*. (Idem.)

A Metz, *le Graoulli*, ou *Kraully*. (*Expilly*, article *Metz*.)

Le dragon de Louvain (*Molanus, Historia Sanctorum imaginum*, p. 506), celui de Ramilies (Le Carpentier, *Hist. de Cambray*, p. 513), celui de St. André, près Villiers, à deux lieues et demie à Vendôme, celui de St. Bertrand de Comminges, et autres."

INDEX.

———◆◇◆———

L

HAYMAN BROTHERS, PRINTERS, GOUGH SQUARE. E.C.

Made in United States
North Haven, CT
07 March 2022

16876570R00104